An Illustrated History of Great Northern Railway Signalling

An Illustrated History of
Great Northern
Railway Signalling

Michael A. Vanns

OPC
Oxford Publishing Co

Contents

First published 2000

ISBN 0 86093 545 0

Published by Oxford Publishing Company

an imprint of Ian Allan Publishing Ltd, Terminal House, Shepperton, Surrey TW17 8AS.
Printed by Ian Allan Printing Ltd, Riverdene Business Park, Hersham, Surrey KT12 4RG.

Code: 0007/B

Front cover:
Photographed in the summer of 1960, the down home signal at Maud Foster signalbox was still a 5ft-long wooden GNR somersault arm with its spectacle and lamp mounted a few feet below. *Trevor Sutcliffe*

Front cover (inset):
Heckington signalbox photographed on 17 April 1973. *Trevor Sutcliffe*

Back cover (top left):
The down signals at Firsby South Junction photographed Easter 1968. *Trevor Sutcliffe*

Back cover (top right):
Egmanton signalbox photographed on 24 October 1976. *Author*

Back cover (bottom):
Claypole signalbox photographed on 3 August 1972. *Author*

Half title page:
Part of the McKenzie & Holland lever frame inside Sykes Junction signalbox, installed in 1885 and photographed on 28 July 1939. The GNR used electrical repeaters very sparingly and of those attached to the block shelf above the levers, only the third from the right, repeating the indication of signal No 4 — the up branch distant — is of GNR origin. *I. W. F. Scrimgeour/Signalling Record Society*

Title page:
Scrooby signalbox was officially opened on 1 January 1872 to control the absolute block sections between Bawtry to the north and Ranskill to the south. In September 1879 the station master at Scrooby was paid an allowance of 2s 6d per week because he was also acting as signalman there. Atlantic No 284, seen here hauling an up express, was built in 1904 and was probably only a few months or even weeks old when this photograph was taken. Scrooby signalbox remained in use until 17 February 1924, when it was closed and replaced by a new one further north at Haworth Colliery sidings. *Great Northern Railway Society Collection*

Foreword

When assembling this illustrated history, I could not help but ask myself: why write a book about a very specialist function of a British railway company that ceased to exist 77 years ago? Who else apart from me would be interested? Inevitably there must be many explanations. Perhaps the simplest is that research for its own sake can be a stimulating pastime, and it is never more rewarding than when the subject has not been studied before. The Great Northern Railway archive at the Public Record Office is a rich seam of raw data easily quarried and, unlike the neighbouring seams of locomotive information which have been worked and reworked for many years, the signalling strata is still largely untouched, nuggets of previously unknown facts still awaiting discovery.

Amassing pure information, however, no matter how precious the individual finds, and making it available to others is not enough, certainly not for this author. To claim this book as a history, the aim has to have been to transform the raw material by interpretation to produce a coherent narrative. The results of interpretation are particularly evident in Chapter 6, the analysis of GNR signalbox types. I do not expect everyone to agree with my findings, and I am sure that even the GNR management itself would have questioned some of the categories, but it is a genuine attempt to try to make sense of a large quantity of unstructured data.

Then there is the wealth of photographic evidence which enhances this history. Images of Patrick Stirling's graceful locomotives, the group of Edwardian station staff posed next to a well-maintained signalbox, and the nodding heads of somersault signals, are reasons enough to produce an illustrated history of the GNR. But this is not a picture book with the photographs reproduced simply to evoke nostalgia. In this book the images are tied in very closely to specific statements in the text and should not be considered independently as mere ornamentation. This is a history with images to illuminate historical arguments.

But there is still another compelling reason why this author chose to examine the signalling practices of a long defunct railway company.

Despite the laudable explanations just outlined, high on the justification list is personal experience and emotion. There is no doubt that for the majority of railway historians, the seeds of a scholarly interest in locomotive design and history were sown at the lineside while train-spotting. For this author an interest in signalling developed from the sights, sounds and smells of GNR equipment still in use long after the society that had created it, and the railway that had needed it, had disappeared. When I first visited Balderton signalbox on the main line just south of Newark-on-Trent in 1972, experiencing the 'Deltics' howling by at 100mph, the building and the lever frame inside it were already a hundred years old. Newark Crossing signalbox was even older and these facts struck me very forcibly. The huge cast-iron posts at Claypole, onto which the pair of 36ft-wide crossing gates were hung, were still proudly marked McKENZIE & HOLLAND, WORCESTER. Why was something made in Worcester planted in the Lincolnshire countryside? I needed to know. All around me was the paraphernalia of another age and by chance I had five impressionable teenage years in which to experience it before it all disappeared.

Since then, as with most railway enthusiasts, I have sought to recapture and explain that past. This illustrated history is not a series of personal reminiscences, however — far from it. It is as academic, historically rigorous, yet as accessible as this author can make it. It is built on fact and analysis, not emotion. But nevertheless, I have to admit that its genesis can be traced back to the experiences of a teenager almost 30 years ago. For many years I have wanted to research and write about Great Northern Railway signalling and fortunately Ian Allan was able to provide the incentive I needed. I have enjoyed every aspect of the task and trust the reader will consider the result was worth the effort.

M. A. Vanns
Coalbrookdale, March 2000

Introduction

The Great Northern Railway (GNR) was incorporated on 26 June 1846 and survived as an independent company until 1 January 1923, when it became part of the London & North Eastern Railway (LNER). It began to operate its first trains from 1 March 1848 on just 30 miles of track between New Holland and Louth, of which a little over half that route was owned by the Manchester, Sheffield & Lincolnshire Railway (MS&LR) and the rest between Grimsby and Louth leased from the East Lincolnshire Railway. By the Grouping of 1923, according to statistics published in the *Railway Magazine*, the GNR operated 1,051 route miles of track. This compared with 1,757 miles owned by its East Coast passenger service partner, the North Eastern Railway (NER); 2,170 miles operated by its great rival, the Midland Railway (MR); 2,667 miles owned by the London & North Western Railway (LNWR) (including the former Lancashire & Yorkshire Railway [L&YR] which had been absorbed the previous year); and 3,005 route miles of the Great Western Railway (GWR), the largest of the pre-Grouping railway companies. In terms of gross receipts, the GNR was ranked fifth after the LNWR, MR, GWR and NER by 1923, moving per annum 31 million passengers and 22 million tons of goods, over half of which was coal. To achieve this, it owned a fleet of 1,359 steam locomotives, a modest total when compared to the MR's figure of 3,019.

But all these statistics, of course, do not tell the whole story, and the 75 years between 1848 and 1923 witnessed the GNR's fortunes ebb and flow in line with those of the country's other great arterial railways. To put what follows into the context of the company's overall history, the reader is recommended to consult one of three good accounts: *The History of the Great Northern Railway*, Charles H. Grinling, Methuen & Co, 1898 and 1903 (with supplementary chapters, George Allen & Unwin, 1966); *The Great Northern Railway*, O. S. Nock, Ian Allan, 1958; *The Great Northern Railway*, John Wrottesley, Batsford, three vols, 1979 and 1981.

As this is also a specialist book, a basic understanding of signalling principles and history has been assumed. A number of books and individual chapters in general railway histories provide this information but it might be worth referring to this author's *abc Signalling in the Age of Steam* (Ian Allan, 1995) and *An Illustrated History of Signalling* (Ian Allan, 1997).

This history is concerned almost entirely with the GNR and very little comment is made of post-1923 work. The author has also not taken up the suggestion of one signalling enthusiast, that block instruments not used by the GNR but often associated in the minds of collectors with the East Coast route should be listed. Lack of space has precluded a detailed survey of signalling on the joint lines in which the GNR had a stake. Signalboxes on the Great Northern & Great Eastern Joint Railway (GN&GEJt) are referred to because they had an effect on the designs elsewhere on the GNR, whereas signalling on the Midland & Great Northern Joint Railway (M&GNRJt) is mentioned only in passing. This is not because it is not of interest but because its story would have biased the main thrust of the text and the subject obviously deserves a history of its own.

For some readers there may also appear to be a lack of measured diagrams in this book but this is due almost entirely to the fact that very few GNR originals survive and the majority of work was carried out by contractors. Of those company drawings that do exist, many are no more than sketches, guidance for joiners, foundrymen and bricklayers. The GNR demanded high standards of its craftsmen and contractors, but it was not as fond of standardisation as was the LNWR, for example (see Richard Foster's excellent *A Pictorial Record of LNWR Signalling*, OPC 1982). The author believes that those GNR drawings reproduced here are representative.

The GNR was very conservative in its approach to signalling and allocated its resources sparingly. Although it conformed to the Board of Trade's latest requirements, it never did more than was necessary and during the first decade of the 20th century it was completely unmoved by the vogue for power signalling embraced enthusiastically by a number of other railway companies. It never manufactured in-house on the same scale as the LNWR, GWR or MR, for example, preferring instead to rely on the products of a number of trusted signalling contractors augmented by small batches of mechanical equipment made in its own district workshops. Nevertheless, as stated in the foreword, the GNR's signalling legacy survived well into living memory, and a substantial amount of mechanical and electrical equipment remained in use perhaps longer than the company itself would have imagined. The following is the story of GNR signalling from 1848 to 1923.

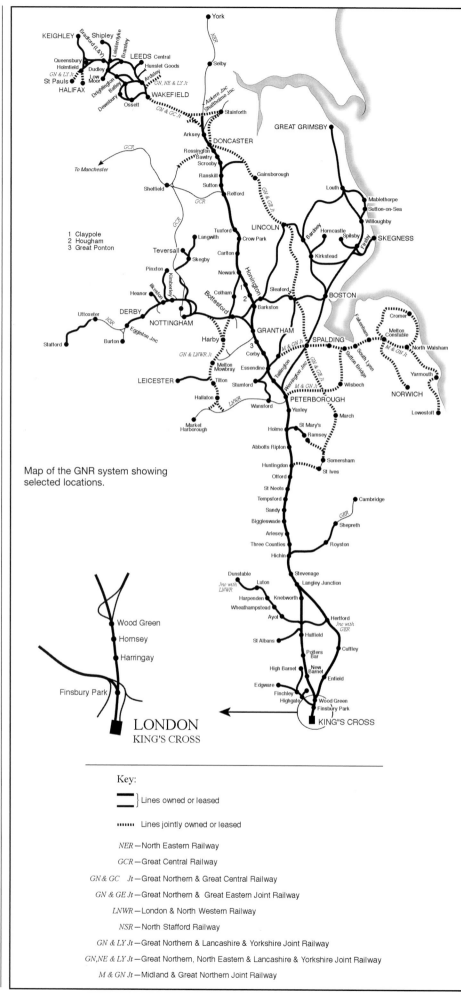

Map of the GNR system showing selected locations.

Key:

━━ } Lines owned or leased

┉┉┉ Lines jointly owned or leased

NER — North Eastern Railway

GCR — Great Central Railway

GN & GC Jt — Great Northern & Great Central Railway

GN & GE Jt — Great Northern & Great Eastern Joint Railway

LNWR — London & North Western Railway

NSR — North Stafford Railway

GN & LY Jt — Great Northern & Lancashire & Yorkshire Joint Railway

GN, NE, LY Jt — Great Northern, North Eastern & Lancashire & Yorkshire Joint Railway

M & GN Jt — Midland & Great Northern Joint Railway

Acknowledgements

For many years, Roger Newman has been painstakingly accumulating information about GNR signalling. His work on this company's history ranks with that for the Midland Railway assembled by John Gough, but whereas the latter's work is well-known and has become widely respected since it was published under the title *A Midland Chronology*, Roger's endeavour remains unpublished and consequently known only to a select few. I could not persuade him to become joint author of this present volume unfortunately, but because he unselfishly shared his knowledge it enabled me to build an historical structure on very sturdy foundations.

Another self-effacing enthusiast who provided invaluable visual raw material for my book is M. A. King. I am enormously grateful that during the 1970s, he had both the nerve and the skill to hang out of the carriage windows of speeding trains and secure well-composed and in focus (!) photographs of both sides of ex-GNR signalboxes as they flashed by. I doubt any other country could breed such men. Without his work, I could not possibly have produced the signalbox typology as it appears in Chapter 6.

For painstakingly reading through my text, missing no historical, spelling or grammatical error, and for questioning almost every non-factual comment I had to make, I must thank Peter Kay of the Signalling Record Society and Signalling Study Group. Conscious of Peter's credentials, it is appropriate here to state that the presentation and interpretation of the information in this book are entirely my own and I take full responsibility for any unwitting inaccuracies of fact.

Another Signalling Record Society member I must thank for reading through and commenting on the text is David Stirling. For providing board and lodging during my frequent visits to the Public Record Office at Kew, I thank Peter Waller of Ian Allan. For allowing me to reproduce items from his collection, I am grateful to Geoff Woodward of the Harpenden Railway Museum.

Thanks also go to the following individuals and organisations who responded to my appeals for information and/or allowed me to use their photographs: Michael Back; Birmingham Central Library; R. K. Blencowe; H. Bonnett; Clifford Buttery; Richard Casserley; Peter Chapman; John Cockcroft; Geoff Goslin; Grantham Library; Great Northern Railway Society (Allan Sibley and Richard Tarpey); Barry Hayward; Historical Model Railway Society; Robert Humm; Lincolnshire Library Service; A. J. Ludlam; National Railway Museum (Ed Bartholomew); Mick Nicholson; North Hertfordshire Museums; Nottingham Local Studies Library; Peterborough Museum & Art Gallery (Elizabeth St Hill Davies); The Public Record Office; Richard Pulleyn; Michael Rakusen; D. N. Robinson OBE; F. W. Shuttleworth; Jack Smith; Signalling Record Society (Keith Spencer responsible for the negatives of Dr Scrimgeour, John Howard-Turner and Colin Betts); Graham Stacey of The Locomotive Club of Great Britain; Trevor J. Sutcliffe; Steve Thompson.

Finally, I must acknowledge the unconditional support I always received from Donald Powell of Birmingham, a signalling enthusiast since the 1920s, who was looking forward to seeing this book in print, but sadly died on 24 April 1999 aged 85.

The Committees

The earliest information about signalling in the GNR's own official records comes from reports submitted by the company's engineer to the Board. The reports commenced in 1847 and continued until the Grouping of 1923. After 1852, when an Executive & Traffic Committee was established, they were considered by that body before Board approval was sought. In 1867 the functions of the former were divided between a Traffic Committee, an Executive Committee and a Way & Works Committee, after which date the engineer's reports went to the latter.

Signalling references appear in the minutes of all these committees and although their brief must have been to concentrate on specific aspects, there was a degree of overlap between them. Usually, the Traffic Committee was responsible for the daily operation of the company's signalling including staffing issues — recommending new appointments and rates of pay to the Board, for example — see Chapter 9. If this committee had any recommendations concerning signalling equipment, they were forwarded to the Way & Works Committee. During the 1870s and 80s, the Executive Committee dealt with fewer signalling matters but when it did, both staffing issues (usually out of the ordinary events such as accidents or appeals) and a few tenders from signalling contractors were minuted, although the majority of the latter were dealt with by the Way & Works Committee. It was the Executive Committee which considered a memorial from London signalmen in the summer of 1875 asking for an alteration in their uniform, for example, and then a few months later decided on the amount of money to be presented to those who 'rendered assistance' at the Abbotts Ripton accident in January 1876.

The Way & Works Committee dealt with signalling installations and equipment, its responsibilities ranging from authorising the acquisition of telegraph wire to overseeing complete resignalling contracts. As mentioned above, it was to this committee that the engineer reported work in progress or completed. Until 1903, the Way & Works Committee recorded every price submitted by every signalling contractor tendering for work anywhere on the GNR. After 1903, only the successful tender was minuted. Chapter 5 examines this in more detail.

The Departments

As with any large organisation, the GNR was divided into a number of departments for operational purposes. By the mid-1880s there were 11 of varying size — Secretaries, Accountants, Traffic, Locomotive, Engineers, Storekeepers, Police, Telegraph, Steamboats Docks & Piers, Canals, and Hotels & Refreshment Rooms. There were three departments which had signalling responsibilities and as at 31 March 1884 these were: the General Manager's and Superintendent of the Line's departments (subdivisions of the Traffic Department); the Engineer's Department; and the Telegraph Department. The Engineer's Department was responsible for constructing and maintaining all but the electrical side of signalling, while the Superintendent's Department employed the signalmen.

General Manager		Superintendent of the Line	
Seymour Clarke	1850-70	John Denniston	1849-53
Henry Oakley	1870-98	Walter Leith	1853-63
C. Steel	1898-1902	John Currey	1863-5
Oliver R. A. Bury	1902-13	Francis Pickersgill Cockshott	1865-95
C. B. D. Dent	1913-22	J. Alexander	1896-1902
		*no post**	*1902-10*
		W. H. Hills	1910-14
		C. J. Selway	1914-22

*Superintendent of the Line post abolished. W. H. Hills became Superintendent of a new Running Department, absorbing some of the responsibilities of the Superintendent of the Line.

Right (2):
Richard Johnson (1827-1924).
Copy of photograph which appeared in the Railway Magazine, *July 1897, p.14.*

Below (4):
Alexander Ross (1845-1923). *Copy of photograph which appeared in the* Railway Magazine, *October 1911, p.334.*

Left (3):
Sir Henry Oakley (1823-1912). *Copy of photograph which appeared in the* Railway Magazine, *September 1910, p.180.*

The Engineers

*Continued as Chief Engineer, Southern Area, London & North Eastern Railway after 1923.

From the beginning, as well as all aspects of civil engineering, permanent way, buildings, etc, signals and all the associated mechanical signalling apparatus were the responsibility of the company's engineer. Only the electric telegraph, and later all electrical signalling equipment, was the responsibility of a Telegraph Superintendent based in Retford. It was not until 1902 that the post of Signal Superintendent was created to oversee the company's signalling, both mechanical and electrical, and advise on new installations — see Chapter 4. Even then the Signal Superintendent reported to the Engineer. That the GNR operated for so long without a company officer or manager dedicated purely to signalling matters is due in no small part to the personality and effectiveness of Richard Johnson, who was the company's Chief Engineer for 35 years from 1861 to 1896.

Born in Spalding, he had joined the GNR in 1847 during the construction of the Loop line through Lincolnshire and became that line's engineer in May 1855. On 30 June 1861 he was promoted to the post of Company Engineer. His career spanned the 'coming of age' of the GNR in all departments, starting from a period when technological advances were still viewed with suspicion and improvements in safety often only made after costly accidents, to an age of supreme mechanical sophistication and confidence, when railway travel had never been safer.

Signalling was only a minor part of the engineering duties Johnson inherited in 1861, which ranged from the building of new lines, the maintenance and continual renewal of permanent way, the replacement of bridges and viaducts, to organising the clearing of blocked drains. Although signalling grew in complexity and importance throughout Johnson's long career, the Board never considered relieving him of that particular responsibility.

Johnson's period in office coincided almost exactly with that of three other long serving and influential company officers. The best known of these men was Patrick Stirling, Locomotive Engineer for 29 years from 1866 to 1895. It was his engines which realised the potential for high speed running along the GNR's main line, a reputation the line has never lost, and it was he who started a tradition of steam locomotive construction at Doncaster that continued through Ivatt, Gresley and Peppercorn until nationalisation. His work has rightly been lauded and is now well documented. But the achievements of Stirling's locomotives were only possible because of the less glamorous and less well-known work of Richard Johnson and two other contemporary colleagues — Francis Pickersgill Cockshott and Henry Oakley.

Francis Cockshott was Superintendent of the Line for 30 years from 1865 to 1895, and Henry Oakley was General Manager for 28 years from 1870 to 1898 *(Picture 3)*. The character of the GNR, its reputation for speed, the location of its signalboxes, stations, and the layout of its sidings, locomotive depots, and marshalling yards was largely of Oakley's, Cockshott's and Johnson's making. Their influence on the way the company was operated was as important as Stirling's on locomotive design and practice.

Numerous letters and reports that passed between these men survive to give some insight into how they worked together. Generally speaking, Oakley dealt directly with the Board, soliciting reports from Cockshott and Johnson, who worked through the committees. Johnson was responsible for providing estimates and the final costings for schemes, then supervising both the contractors' and the GNR's own labour. On some construction jobs, such as the building of the Newark to Bottesford Branch between 1876 and 1878, for example, a 'project' engineer would be employed, the GNR turning frequently to John Fraser of Leeds until his death in September 1881.

From the surviving documentation Johnson comes across as a hard working man who took a cautious approach to every job he was involved with, preferring pragmatic solutions to the implementation of grand plans. This characteristic was both a response to and a reflection of the GNR Board's own management ethos but it also meant that changes of plan often involved the company in extra expenditure. The records also show that he was not a man who liked confrontation and he was careful in his dealings with Oakley, who was obviously a more forceful character. Just one example illustrates this. In February 1870, when John Saxby was petitioning for a prolongation of his 1856 'interlocking' patent (No 1479), Johnson wrote to Oakley commenting:

'I am very much inclined to think that after all it will be well for us as a Company, not to move against renewal of Messrs Saxby & Farmer's patents — at this moment, we do not pay any royalty to any Signal-making firm whatever, and probably if we oppose a renewal of the patent now, we may bring upon ourselves the hostility of patentees, and give us no end of work.'

Oakley disagreed completely, and was actively involved in fighting Saxby's case along with representatives from the GWR, LNWR, South Eastern Railway (SER), London Brighton & South Coast Railway (LBSCR), McKenzie & Holland and Stevens & Sons, all of whom shared the costs of the Judicial Review on 17 June 1870. As a result, Saxby's petition was dismissed.

Johnson's reference to patentees stemmed from the fact that he was at this time going some way towards providing the GNR with an in-house mechanical signalling equipment manufacturing capacity, the products of which might, at this period of intense competition in the signalling industry, be regarded as infringements of patents taken out by others. These attempts at self-sufficiency, however, were soon over-whelmed by the amount of work necessary to modernise the company's signalling. In March 1871 Johnson apologetically asked the Way & Works Committee's permission to buy locking frames for Doncaster from Easterbrook & Co '...because we are so busy in our own signal shops preparing locking apparatus for the New Lines, and also for the extension of the Block working...' In January 1872 he was pleased to report that all the signals and lever frames for use on the Barnet Extension were being made in the GNR's London workshops, but a month later he obviously felt an explanation was needed for employing Saxby & Farmer at Peterborough. He commented:

'I should have been glad to have dealt with this work in our own shops in London, but owing to the pressure which now arises in connection with the ordinary maintenance of signals and the extension of the Block System, I find we are unable to deal with some of the large alterations so rapidly as is desirable.'

Johnson had offices at Peterborough situated in The Crescent and in July 1872, he proposed moving the manufacture of switches and crossings and the maintenance of signals to a new building on the northeast side of the passenger station, '...so that [the Engineer] will be able to exercise a still more strict supervision...' In November 1873, he reported that the provision of new locking apparatus and signals was forcing him to employ more men and a screw-cutting lathe and a planing and drilling machine would be needed for these workshops. For the Lincolnshire, or Boston, District manufacturing of signalling equipment was undertaken at Boston, and in the first week of January the following year Johnson was asking for a slotting machine for these works '...the use of which will save much manual labor [sic] and so repay the necessary original outlay in about 12 months'. Although nowhere in the company's records is there a direct appeal from Johnson to set up a signalling department, it was during this period that reference was made to the GNR becoming wholly self-sufficient in the making and installation of signals. At the same Way & Works Committee meeting on 16 April 1874 when this was mentioned, Johnson also reported that from then on he wanted to purchase locking frames only from Ransomes & Rapier. However, three weeks later, the same committee gave its approval for McKenzie & Holland to signal the Canonbury Extension because the engineer's shops were so busy.

At the beginning of 1875, the Way & Works Committee approved the plan for a Signal & Carpenters Shop at Peterborough but it is not clear whether this was an extension of the existing facilities or a completely new workshop. The GNR did manufacture a few dozen lever frames, as is discussed later, but what is certain is that it never established a signalling works on the scale of the LNWR's at Stockport and Crewe or the GWR's at Reading, for example. We will probably never know whether it was because Johnson was unwilling to see it happen, or because he did not grasp the opportunity he was given by the Way & Works Committee. Perhaps he believed the Board would never agree to the considerable initial outlay that would be needed. In the event, the use of contractors for most new work was resumed in the mid-1870s and Johnson found himself supervising a number of different firms as they continued with the task of interlocking all junctions and main stations on the system. As interlocking spread, the financial implications of maintaining (with the GNR's own men) the increasing number of signals and signalboxes obviously concerned him deeply, and in March 1876 Johnson reported:

'The maintenance of Signals, Locking apparatus and connections has now become a very serious additional expense to the Company and I do not see at present any means of reducing this expenditure. The signals are increased so much in number and the connections are so much more complicated than they were in early days, that this part of our work, must, I fear, continue to increase seriously, as we have not only to provide the signals, but they must be kept in the highest state, so as to ensure perfect working; and the number of men required for this purpose is very large.'

As was the case throughout his career, Johnson was always cost-conscious and careful to justify any expenditure that might appear profligate.

Patrick Stirling died in office on 1 November 1895 (aged 76), and at the end of the following month Cockshott retired at the age of 71. Johnson followed exactly a year later on 31 December 1896, aged 70, and in March 1898 Sir Henry Oakley retired at the age of 75. That all these men's careers should have ended within months of each other was significant, because it not only marked the end of arguably the most exciting and prosperous era in the GNR's history but it also allowed new blood into the operational heart of the company. The new locomotive engineer, H. A. Ivatt, was recruited from the Great Southern & Western Railway in Ireland; Charles Steel from the Highland Railway stepped into Henry Oakley's shoes, and Johnson was replaced by Alexander Ross *(Picture 4)* from the MS&LR. Only Cockshott's successor was a GNR man — John Alexander — but he was soon succeeded by Oliver Bury who, although related to the company's first General Manager, had made a reputation for himself in South America. Locomotive development still had a long way to go but with the benefit of hindsight so far as engineering and mechanical signalling were concerned, all the exciting developments were over.

Districts and Divisions

Until the 'Towns Line' opened in 1852 — completing the main line between King's Cross and Doncaster — for operational and maintenance purposes the GNR was seen as one unit. The first subdivision came in April 1853, when two proto-District Engineers were appointed, reporting to the Company Engineer, Joseph Cubitt. Henry Carr took charge of the main line and Walter Marr Brydone the Loop line (through Boston) and the East Lincolnshire Railway. Their salaries were £400pa. From May 1855 W. C. Graves took over responsibility for the main line and Richard Johnson was appointed as engineer of the Loop and East Lincolnshire lines. When Brydone succeeded Cubitt in 1856, three new Districts were created with their own District Engineers. The main line from London

to Peterborough was placed under R. Gastenau, the section from Peterborough to Askern and the Grantham-Nottingham branch was allotted to W. C. Graves, with Richard Johnson retaining his responsibilities for the Loop and East Lincolnshire lines and the Horncastle branch which the GNR ran for an independent company.

In 1861 Johnson succeeded W. M. Brydone as Chief Engineer and three years later he recommended dividing the main and loop lines into six new districts:

> London to Stevenage
> Hitchin to Holme
> Peterborough to Claypole
> Newark to Askern
> Peakirk to Gainsborough
> Boston to Grimsby

Whether this recommendation was implemented or not and, if it was, how long these groupings survived, is not known. What adds to the historical confusion during this decade and for many years thereafter, is the fact that engineering districts differed from operating ones. Signalmen and engine crews would have recognised different boundaries all over the system.

Concentrating on the Engineer's Department because it was responsible for the mechanical side of the company's signalling, during the 1860s and '70s, the districts were responsible for building signalboxes, limited manufacturing and installation, as well as maintenance. This resulted in a great deal of variation in structures and equipment between districts (see Chapter 6). Manufacture was very much a bespoke process based on carpentry, simple foundry work and blacksmithing. Signals were probably made in every district, the shops at London and Boston, for example, having been mentioned already, and in the early 1870s and again between the end of the 1880s and the early years of the 20th century, a number of lever frames were also made in-house — see Chapter 2.

The work of the District Engineers' teams often overlapped with that of signalling contractors, and there are instances where the job of constructing signalboxes along a section of line was divided between contractors and company labour. For example, on the first section of the Derbyshire Extension lines in 1875, the tender document stated that, 'The GNR Co. will build one signalbox at each station, all

other signalboxes are to be built by the contractor...'

By the end of the 1870s, there were five districts: London, Grantham, Boston, Notts & Derby and West Riding & Yorkshire. The boundary between the London and Grantham Districts was Werrington Junction. Between then and the end of the 1890s, the districts were reorganised at least once, so that by the beginning of the 20th century they were as follows:

> Main Line
> Lincolnshire District
> Nottinghamshire, Derbyshire &
> Leicestershire District
> West Riding, Yorkshire District

The districts were subdivided into sections, and by the 1890s district engineers had a department of one or more signal inspectors, who were in turn responsible for a number of locking-frame mechanics, signal linesmen, chargemen and labourers. The number of staff in a particular district depended on the number of lever frames, working levers and signals in each section.

Routine maintenance within a district was a self-contained departmental task but when significant alterations were required, for example the resiting of signals, a site meeting took place with representatives from the Traffic and the Engineer's Departments. Weekly, monthly and other returns, documenting all signalling work carried out in a district, were completed by the signal inspectors on specially printed forms and submitted to their district engineers, who in turn added their own comments before passing them on to the Chief Engineer.

These arrangements led to a good deal of autonomy within districts, and three years after Johnson's retirement his successor, Alexander Ross, tried in 1899 to bring some common purpose to the districts by appointing a peripatetic 'signalling assistant' whose job it was to visit every one with instructions from headquarters. Ross introduced further reforms in 1902 which are examined in detail below (Signal Superintendent) and this date was also significant because it was the year when administrative changes led to the reconstitution of the districts into four divisions, which remained until the GNR was absorbed into the LNER in 1923:

Main Line Division
  King's Cross to Shaftholme Junction
  High Barnet Branch (Finsbury Park to High Barnet)
  Edgware Branch (Finchley Junction to Edgware)
  Enfield Branch (Wood Green *[Picture 5]* to Enfield, extended through to Langley Junction in 1918)
  St Albans Branch (Hatfield to St Albans Junction)
  Hertford Branch (Hatfield to Hertford)
  Hatfield, Luton and Dunstable Branch
  Hitchin & Cambridge Branch
  Holme & Ramsey Branch
  Fletton Branch
  Stamford Branch (Essendine to Stamford)
  Wansford Branch Sibson Extension (Stamford Junction to Wansford)

Eastern Division (formerly the old Lincolnshire District)
  Loop Line (Werrington Junction to Pyewipe Junction, Lincoln)
  Horncastle Branch (Kirkstead Junction to Horncastle) (GN&GE Joint Railway)
  East Lincolnshire Line (Boston to Grimsby Goods Junction)
  Louth & Bardney Branch
  Skegness Branch (Firsby South Junction to Skegness)
  Spilsby Branch (Firsby Junction to Spilsby)
  Willoughby & Louth Branch (via Sutton-on-Sea and Mablethorpe)
  Essendine & Bourne Branch (Essendine to Bourne)
  Bourne & Sleaford Branch
  Grantham, Sleaford & Boston Branch (Barkston Junction to Boston)
  Grantham & Lincoln Branch (Honington Junction *(Picture 6)* to Pelham Street Junction, Lincoln)

Western Division (formerly the old Nottinghamshire, Derbyshire & Leicestershire District)
  Grantham & Nottingham Branch
  Woolsthorpe Branch (Belvoir Junction to Denton Ironstone Siding)
  Nottingham Suburban Line (Trent Lane Junction to Daybrook Junction)
  Trent Lane West Junction to Weekday Cross Junction, Nottingham
  Nottingham Victoria station (jointly owned with GCR)
  Stafford & Derbyshire Lines (Colwick West Junction to Egginton Junction, NSR and Bromshall Junction, NSR to Stafford Junction, LNWR)
  Leen Valley Line and extensions (Leen Valley Junction to Annesley Junction, GCR and Kirkby Junction, GCR to Langwith Junction, LD&ECR)
  Erewash Valley Lines — Pinxton Branch (Awsworth Junction to Pinxton)
  Heanor Branch (Stanton Junction to Heanor)
  Stanton Branch
  Newark & Bottesford Line
  Waltham, Eaton and Eastwell Branches
  Leicester Line (Marefield Junction to Leicester)
  GN&LNW Joint Railway (GNR responsible for signalling north of Melton Mowbray)

West Riding Division
  Doncaster, Wakefield and Ardsley to Leeds Central
  Leeds Low Level (GN&NE Joint Lines)
  Hunslet Branch (Beeston Junction to Hunslet Goods)
  Barnby Don Branch (Adwick Junction to Bramwith)
  Methley Joint Line (Lofthouse Junction to Methley)
  Wakefield (Balne Lane Junction) to Ossett, Dewsbury, Batley and Adwalton Junction
  Ossett to Batley (via Chickenley)
  Batley & Beeston Branch
  Ardsley to Laisterdyke (via Gildersome)
  Holbeck to Laisterdyke and Bradford *(Picture 7)* (via Stanningley)
  Shipley Branch (Laisterdyke Junction to Shipley)
  Bramley to Lowmoor
  St Dunstan's to Keighley
  Queensbury and Halifax Branches
  Halifax & Ovenden Line
  Laisterdyke to Halifax (via Bowling)

Another change which occurred in 1902 also affected the way in which signalling was dealt with. In that year, the post of Chief Traffic Manager was created and occupied by W. J. Grinling, who stayed in post until 1919. Between these dates he reported to the Traffic Committee on signalling matters in place of the General Manager.

Telegraph Superintendent

Whereas the mechanical and structural aspects of signalling were the province of the Engineer's Department acting through the district engineers, the electrical equipment was the responsibility of the Telegraph Department at Retford. The first reference to the department is in a circular from Francis Cockshott dated 15 July 1867, drawing attention to the reporting of any defects in telegraph instruments to the local telegraph lineman and Mr Radcliffe, the Telegraph Superintendent at Retford. At this date Radcliffe was not a GNR employee but worked for the Magnetic Telegraph Co, who maintained the company's telegraphs under contract. Two years later on 15 November 1869, the Way & Works Committee approved the drawings and estimates submitted by the General Manager for

'...an office and a shed for stores which he recommends should be erected at Retford for the accommodation of the Electrician and his staff who will maintain the Company's Telegraph system after 1 January 1870 — the estimated cost being £285.14.11...'

Telegraph Superintendents
James Radcliffe [1]   10.1870-6.1892
Thomas Ireland   5.7.1893-31.12.1912
Frederick Downes   1.1.1913-1922*
Starting salary £350pa; continued in post after the Grouping

On 18 October 1870 Radcliffe was appointed as the GNR's first Telegraph Superintendent, and as with many senior managers, he had a long career with the company, remaining in post until his death on 2 June 1892. At the beginning of 1882 his salary was raised from £350 to £400pa for '...efficient services rendered'. During his tenure at Retford, he took out a number of patents for signalling equipment which are examined in Chapter 3.

Signal Superintendent

Signal Superintendents
W. H. Cannon   3.1902-6.1920
A. E. Tattersall   6.1920-1922*
* Continued in post after the Grouping of 1923 as Assistant Signal Engineer, Southern Area LNER.

As mentioned above, this post was created in 1902 following the recommendations of the then Engineer, A. Ross. On 28 February that year he produced a typewritten report (itself a sign of modernisation within the company as reports until then had almost always been handwritten) for consideration by the Way & Works Committee meeting of 6 March 1902. His opening paragraph read:

'Gentlemen, For some time I have been impressed with the necessity of a change being brought about in connection with the section of the Engineering Department dealing with the Signalling of the Line, with the view of ensuring uniformity in the appliances used, and a better and more systematic attention as regards maintaining and keeping the various parts clean, lubricated, and in good working order.'

After explaining existing practices, he continued:

'...I am satisfied that the time has now arrived when the company should appoint a Signal Superintendent acting under the Engineer, and

[1] James Radcliffe was born in Stockport in 1831 or 1832.

responsible to him for the proper condition of the Signalling Appliances generally, including the Locking-Frames, Signals, Connections and all the Mechanical Appliances, and qualified to undertake the following duties:

1. The preparation of general plans of Stations and Sidings
2. The preparation of Signal-Diagrams
3. The preparation of detail drawings of all Signalling Appliances, and the drawing up of Specifications and Bills of Quantities for Works to be let by Contract
4. The preparation of Locking-Tables
5. The superintendence of the carrying out of all Signalling Works
6. The measuring up of work during execution and when completed; and the preparation of Monthly Certificates and Final Accounts
7. With sufficient mechanical knowledge to keep himself acquainted with new appliances and new systems, such as Power Signalling proposals.'

To reinforce the authority of the new Superintendent, Ross went on to propose that he:

'...be empowered to place himself in communication with the Signal Inspectors to request them to meet him when inspecting Signalling on various parts of the line, and the Inspectors to take instructions from him, they reporting to the District Engineers, if necessary.'

The signal plans were to be submitted to both the Superintendent of the Line and the Locomotive Engineer, a procedure which appears to have been in place already but was not always carried out. Once the plans had been approved by the Board, Ross requested that representatives of the Superintendent of the Line, the Locomotive Engineer and the District Engineer should make a site visit to finalise the details. After the post of Superintendent of the Line ceased to exist from the end of 1902, a representative from the new Running Department was consulted in his place.

Board approval for Ross's suggested changes and the new appointment was forthcoming on 28 April 1902 and the person chosen to be the first Superintendent was W. H. Cannon. Aged 44, he had been working for the GNR for the past 15 years on signalling work between London and Peterborough. It was agreed to raise his salary from £286 to £325, and the Board was assured that this was the only additional cost necessary in creating this new post.

That this appointment should come in 1902 indicates that A. Ross was well aware of the latest developments in signalling and how conservative the GNR had become in this department. By then pneumatic, electro-pneu-matic and all-electric systems were being embraced enthusiastically by a number of British railway companies. The LNWR had developed its own all-electric power signalling system at Crewe in 1897/8; the GNR's partner in the East Coast route, the NER, had on trial a McKenzie & Holland electro-pneumatic system on the Tyne, the London & South Western Railway (LSWR) was experimenting with pneumatic automatic signalling, and the Great Central Railway (GCR) was only two years away from bringing an impressive widening and power signalling scheme into operation on its busy lines east of Manchester. Ross, of course, had come from the MS&LR before it had been renamed the GCR.

Despite the potential to modernise GNR signalling practice, however, Cannon made no revolutionary changes. When automatic signals were considered to deal with the exceptionally heavy bank holiday traffic along the Skegness line in 1904, the idea was dismissed as too expensive. What progress was made was firmly in the company's long-standing tradition of pragmatism (see Chapter 2). Cannon remained in post until June 1920, dying shortly after his retirement after 49 years in the company's employ.

The appointment which could have transformed GNR signalling practice if it had been made earlier, occurred in 1920 when A. E. Tattersall replaced Cannon as Signal Superintendent. Tattersall was not a 'company man' but had come from the Metropolitan Railway. There he had no reservations in using the latest technologies, particularly track circuiting, and had embraced new theories from the USA, experimenting with colour-light signals and 'three-position' light signals. In 1921 he published *Modern Developments in Railway Signalling* and presented a paper to the Institution of Railway Signal Engineers (IRSE) entitled *Three Position Signalling* which was hugely influential in the development of interwar signalling practice.

Unfortunately, Tattersall's time with the GNR was too short to effect any radical changes, and although his responsibilities for GNR signalling continued when he became Assistant Signal Engineer (Southern Area) for the LNER in 1923, his subsequent promotion in 1928 to the North Eastern Area of the system based at York meant that that part of the system reaped the benefits of his talents (see *British Railway Signalling*, O. S. Nock, George Allen & Unwin, 1969). The LNER concentrated its investment in Tattersall's innovations on the former NER, and this was one of the main reasons why signalling on former GNR lines remained fundamentally unaltered until the 1970s.

Above right (6):
Honington Junction station as it appeared in the first decade of the 20th century. The photograph clearly shows the 1870s/80s practice of placing the signal spectacle and lamp several feet below the semaphore arm. The signalbox shown here was brought into use on 25 October 1875, replacing the 1860s structure shown in *Picture 103.*
Peterborough Museum & Art Gallery

Right (7):
Hammerton Street Junction, Bradford, photographed in September 1969, was a good example of a Type 1b/Top Lights design of signalbox. It opened in 1882 and was closed on 16 September 1979. *M. A. King*

2. Block Working and Interlocking

For most of the 20th century, the relationship between block working and interlocking was an intimate one, and one that has been taken for granted. All over the country, hundreds of signalboxes with tens and sometimes hundreds of levers working signals, some almost a mile away, as well as the majority of points within a radius of 350 yards, also contained the necessary electrical instruments to regulate the passage of trains approaching and leaving their area of control. But this has not always been the case, and on the GNR, as elsewhere, it was not until the 1870s that block working and interlocking were fully brought together and the relationship formalised to leave a legacy of exhaustive and rigorously enforced regulations which remained operative for the next hundred years.

In the 1850s, signalling was seen by the GNR in three distinct compartments: the first was the use of semaphores (see Chapter 4) at passenger stations to control the trains passing through, which was the responsibility of policemen or signalmen or sometimes porters; the second was the working of both signals and points at junctions, which was a signalman's task *(Picture 8)*; and the third was the use of the electric telegraph to supplement the fixed signals and to communicate between passenger stations to ascertain what trains were due and when, a responsibility originally given to station masters.

With the introduction of the block system between London and Hatfield in 1854, signalmen were put in charge of the telegraph instruments as well as the fixed signals, and in the following decade more points at stations and yards were also placed under their control. As with points at junctions, there was no way of interlocking them with the main signals until John Saxby patented his 'simultaneous motion' equipment in 1856. Ten years elapsed before interlocking at junctions became an issue for the GNR, due in part to pressure exerted by the Board of Trade. Even then, it was not considered necessary to interlock the majority of points and signals at stations and yards and bring them under the direct control of signalboxes. The evidence shows that after important junctions had been interlocked by the end of the 1860s, the priority in the first two years of the 1870s was extending the block system. It was only after this had been achieved throughout the main line that attention turned back to interlocking, the General Manager's report of September 1873 stating, '...the time has arrived when he thinks it is desirable to extend the application of the Locking Apparatus to all points of importance on the Great Northern system...'

What had helped delay the spread of interlocking was the resistance of Richard Johnson, the company's Engineer, to 'complicated' machinery. His change of heart was recorded in the notes of the debate which took place after Richard Rapier had delivered his paper, *On the Fixed Signals of Railways* to the Institution of Civil Engineers in March 1874. Johnson recalled:

'...For the last 13 or 14 years he had been almost every day carefully considering this question of locking apparatus or no locking apparatus... He had, as far as he could, opposed the introduction of locking apparatus, but it was now only fair to admit, that in his opinion, every set of switches which communicated in any way with the main line should be under the control of a signalman, and that it should be out of the power of any shunter or porter to alter those switches at will. It therefore came to this, that more or less, locking apparatus was a necessity.'

In just 10 years between 1866 and 1876, the GNR's signalling changed more dramatically — and fundamentally — than at any other period in the company's history, and the chronology outlined above is important in putting the information in this chapter into perspective.

Above (8):
This Stevens & Sons stirrup frame operating the four semaphores at Gullet Junction, just south of Doncaster station, was installed in the 1860s. The photograph is a good record of the sort of simple apparatus the GNR employed to regulate the movement of trains at junctions before Board of Trade pressure led to the use of more sophisticated interlocking lever frames. To the left of the signalman were the point levers, not interconnected or interlocked with the stirrups, and all this equipment was positioned, in the open, on top of a signalling stage approximately 20ft high. This official GNR photograph was taken in the late 1880s to record equipment which was by then completely outdated. It was finally taken out of use on 3 February 1895. (See also *Picture 97*.)
Peterborough Museum & Art Gallery

Block Working on the Main Line: 1854-76

The electric telegraph was not used on the main line until 1852 and at first it was not viewed as part of the GNR's signalling system. After an accident at Hornsey on 31 August 1853, when the Board of Trade recommended it should supplement the use of fixed signals, Seymour Clarke, the GNR's General Manager, commented,

'...it is at present impracticable to carry this suggestion into effect — the GNR Company not being the owners, and having the use only of two of the wires of the Telegraph; but, so soon as the arrangements now in course of being concluded with the Telegraph Co. are completed... this suggestion of the Board of Trade [will] be further considered...'

This did not take long and in February 1854 Clarke reported that having protected the company's tunnels with the telegraph and the 'In and Out' system, '...he can easily try the plan of signalling all trains from station to station between London and Hatfield — but which will require the addition of 11 men to the staff, as Signalmen'. This was achieved and two years later this 'space interval' system of working trains, which was eventually refined to become block working, was extended from Hatfield to Hitchin.

From then onwards the new system worked well and it was only after February 1858, when the MR opened its extension to Hitchin and its trains began to share the GNR's tracks into the capital, that it started to cause delays. At the end of 1860 the system was modified so that more than one train travelling in the same direction could be allowed between 'signal stations' except where there was a tunnel (see Chapter 3 for further details). One of the justifications for this change was to bring the system in line with that used on the LNWR. The first few years of the new decade were ones of financial stringencies but there was steady growth in the number and the speed of trains, for which the GNR maintained its reputation. Grinling noted in his *History* that the crisis which affected every railway company in 1866 was weathered by the GNR, which was just as well, because a dramatic accident in Welwyn Tunnel on 9 June that year, and growing pressure from the Board of Trade and the public, ultimately involved the company in a huge outlay on the upgrading of its signalling over the next 10 years.

The chain of events which led to disaster at Welwyn started when a down empty coal train became disabled inside the tunnel. Unaware of this, the signalman allowed an MR goods train to follow it and the resulting collision was compounded when an up goods train carrying meat ran into the wreckage. The remains of the three trains burned uncontrollably for over 15 hours. This accident had an immediate effect on the working of other tunnels on the network not protected by the block system, and within days it was agreed to spend £28 substituting the 'In and Out' system between Peascliffe Tunnel (just north of Grantham) and Barkston Junction with block working. But the most significant results of the accident were the decisions to introduce new block instruments which could show permanent indications to the signalman, and the re-

establishment of what was by then called absolute block working between London and Hitchin. Numerous new signal stations were erected to ensure the absolute block sections were of a length which did not delay trains, as Richard Johnson's reports to the Way & Works Committee make clear.

On the main line north of Hitchin, block working was still only in force at a few places at the end of the 1860s. A report drawn up after a special Station Committee comprising members of the GNR Board had visited various places on the system during September 1868 shows that senior management still considered block working was only needed at especially dangerous or congested areas and had not grasped the wider safety implications. At Shelford they looked at the signalling '...in reference to the suggestion recently made that the block system of telegraphing should be applied at certain places where the line was curved, or a fast train following a slow train could not be well seen.' A decision to introduce block working there was deferred. They visited Arlesey and thought the curves at Offord were very sharp, but made no decision about the upgrading of the signalling at either place. At Peterborough they were more positive and agreed block working should be introduced between Peacock Bridge to the south and Walton level crossing to the north[2], but at Grantham they were unsure and once again made no decision.

A few months later at the end of 1868, block working from Grantham Junction on the main line to and through Gonerby Tunnel on the branch to Nottingham was put in hand, but the circumstances of an accident which occurred at Retford on 28 February 1869 is a very good illustration that the importance of concentrating all signals and points and the electric telegraph

[2] *Walton Crossing was not made a 'block signal station' until the very end of 1873 when the gatemen were replaced by two Third Class signalmen.*

instruments under a signalman's control had still not been fully appreciated by the Board, or if it had, then financial considerations made members believe it could be ignored. On the up main line just north of Retford station there was a shunting signal capable of showing either caution or all clear. It was positioned between the up distant signal to the north and the station semaphore to the south, which were worked from the tower signalbox at the station (semaphores are examined in detail in Chapter 4). The shunting signal was worked by those undertaking the shunting and it was neither interlocked with the main signals nor worked from the tower signalbox, which meant, as during the early morning of the accident, it could be put to caution to protect a shunting movement on the main line while the two up main semaphore signals either side of it were showing all clear. On this occasion the up Scotch Mail Train ran past the all clear signals into the shunting engine still at work on the main line.

This accident undoubtedly helped the arguments for improved signalling and in June 1869 Johnson reported to the Board as to the extent of block signalling on its lines — see Table 1 — along with the implications of extending it over the entire system.

To complete the block system on the main line, all branches (both double and single track) and the GNR's responsibilities in the West Riding, the report concluded that 271 extra staff,

Table 1. Block working in operation, June 1869	
Main line	
King's Cross to Hitchin South Jct	31 miles 60 chains
Peacock Bridge, Peterborough to Crescent Jct, Peterborough	61 chains
Spittal Jct, Peterborough to Werrington Jct	2 miles 71 chains
Peascliffe Tunnel Box to Barkston Jct	1 mile 74 chains
Rossington to Bridge Jct, Doncaster	4 miles 8 chains
Edgware branch	
Edgware Branch Jct to East End Finchley	3 miles 17 chains
Grantham and Nottingham line	
Grantham Jct to Barrowby signalbox	1 mile 74 chains
West Riding	
West Riding Jct, Wakefield Westgate to Holbeck	9 miles 64 chains
Wortley East Jct to Mill Lane Jct	7 miles 73 chains
Wortley South Jct to Wortley West Jct	23 chains

162 new signal stations, 132 additional signals, 1,038 extra block instruments and 519 extra block bells would be required.

Perhaps because of the daunting and, more significantly, the expensive task highlighted by the report, improvements continued to be carried out in a piecemeal fashion. In May 1870, Johnson drew up plans for the introduction of block working through Newark utilising five signal huts that had only recently been erected at Barnby, Newark South, Newark North, Midland Crossing (*Picture 9*) and Muskham. At the beginning of June the Traffic Committee agreed that block working should be introduced between Marsh Gate, Doncaster and Shaftholme Junction, where the NER's new line from York via Selby would make its connection with the GNR. It was also recommended that '...the NER and L&YR companies be pressed to extend the block system from Shaftholme to Moss and Askern respectively.'

But the pressure to extend block working comprehensively was becoming irresistible and that summer Johnson was instructed to prepare a plan and estimates for protecting the line between Hitchin and Peterborough. These were completed on 28 October 1870 and immediately given Board approval.

The final impetus to complete block working along the whole of the main line was provided in a robust report presented by Henry Oakley, General Manager, to the Board on 28 January 1871. In this he drew attention to the MR's intention to introduce the system on its lines and then went on to say:

'...It is probable that Companies employing the Block System, or doubling their line, may convey a more favourable impression on the score of safety than other companies that do not adopt either one of these courses, and though I cannot present either to you as an absolute preventive against accidents, I am bound to admit that the security of running trains will be very much enhanced by the Extension of the Absolute Block System over your line between London and Doncaster.'

Conveying 'a more favourable impression' upon the general public made good commercial sense but Oakley was obviously also aware of the effect the new powers to be granted to the Board of Trade by the Regulation of Railways Act in November that year would have on all railway companies. The right of inspection of new lines was being extended to alterations on existing lines as well and consequently the views of the Railway Inspectorate were assuming more importance.

Table 3. Requirements for block working, January 1871

Requirements	Werrington Jct-Grantham	Hougham-Rossington*
New signalboxes	8	12
Extra signals	15	24
Extra block instruments	48	80
Extra block bells	24	40
Six-plate batteries	48	80
12-plate batteries	24	40
Three-wire Telegraph on existing poles	25 miles 76 chains	38 miles 72 chains

*By January 1871, as well as the stretches of line noted in the 1869 report, block working had been brought into operation between Grantham and Hougham, and between Tuxford station and Lincoln Road Crossing.

On 3 February 1871 the Board gave its approval, agreeing to spend £2,412 13s 9d installing the block system throughout on the stretch of line between Werrington Junction and Grantham, and £3,749 14s 6d for its extension from there to Rossington. The yearly outlay for signalmen and apparatus was estimated at £3,700. By the beginning of 1871 work had already started between Hitchin and Peterborough, Johnson reporting on 30 January that block working had progressed as far as Sandy and new signal huts were nearly complete at Barford and Offord. At the end of March he noted that the framing for four huts needed between Abbotts Ripton and Peterborough was being prepared at Hitchin. These were either temporary structures to bring the block system into operation as soon as possible or the first of a new generation of GNR signalboxes large enough to accommodate not only the block instruments but interlocking lever frames as well (see Chapter 6). Certainly Johnson's report of 30 June 1871 seems to imply the latter was the case at Wood Walton, Conington and Yaxley, because unlike elsewhere in his text, the fixing of locking apparatus is specifically mentioned in relation to these places, and it needed something more substantial that a temporary signal hut. May 1871 witnessed block working in operation over the 32 miles between Hitchin and Abbotts Ripton and it would be completed to Peterborough by August that year (*Picture 10*).

On the section of main line north of Peterborough between Werrington Junction and Doncaster, the same frantic efforts were being made. On this section of line temporary huts

Table 2. Estimated cost of block telegraphs from Hitchin North box to Peacock Bridge (Peterborough), 28 October 1870

Additional equipment	Initial outlay	Yearly outlay stores	maintenance	renewal
9 signalboxes	£900	£105 2s 3d	£11 6s 6d	£45
18 signals	£900	£96 7s 6d	£32 5s	£75
76 block instruments and fixing	£307 16s		£26 12s	£29 2s 8d
38 block bells and fixing	£159 12s		£6 13s	£17 14s 8d
76 six-plate batteries	£38	£39 18s	£1 18s	£3 16s
38 12-plate batteries	£28 10s	£26 12s	£1 8s 6d	£2 17s
43 miles 15 chains of three-wire telegraph on existing poles	£874 10s 11d		£37 15s 9d	£43 3s 9d
Proportion of poles			£38 17s 5d	£22 2s 8d
Total	**£3,208 8s 11d**			
5% on first cost of £3,208 8s 11d				£160 8s 5d
15 signalmen, wages, including clothes and bonus				£1,050
Total (stores + maintenance + renewals + signalmen)				**£1,874 1s 1d**

Left (10):
One of the few photographs of an early 1870s signalbox, is this one taken at Stevenage station in the late 1880s. The 1871 signalbox was replaced in 1898.
Bucknall Collection/Ian Allan Library

Right (11):
Egmanton signalbox was located just south of Tuxford, between Newark and Retford. The signalbox was an example of the Type 1a/Balderton design. Just visible on the opposite side of the crossing is the small wooden signal hut which probably predated the signalbox by only a few months. It has been suggested that the post on which the up and down semaphore arms were fixed originally passed through the square hole at the apex of the roof. The photograph was taken on 7 November 1964, looking north.
H. B. Priestley/Nottingham Local Studies Library

Below right (12):
Considering Bell Bar signalbox closed c1882 after only 10 years in use, this photograph is indeed a lucky survivor. The rectangular board with a semicircular top hung beneath the operating room windows indicated to passing linesmen whether or not the telegraph instruments needed attention. At present there is no explanation as to why there were two doors into the locking room.
Great Northern Railway Society

were erected prior to the building of more substantial signalboxes, along with the fitting of the necessary block instruments into comparatively new timber signalboxes, for example at Grantham Junction, Barkston Junction and through Newark as mentioned above. The block system at the latter had been scheduled to be brought into use in April 1871 but it was delayed and was not operational until early June. By September Johnson could tell the Way & Works Committee that the system had been completed between Grantham and Tuxford, controlled from 12 signal stations. If other official records are correct, then almost half of these must have been temporary huts and there appears to be photographic evidence for this. The photograph of Egmanton signalbox (*Picture 11*), which was just south of Tuxford, shows the brick-based signalbox opened on 17 November 1871, and on the opposite side of the tracks a wooden hut which was probably one of those 12 signal stations. Finally, in January 1872, Johnson reported that the separate sections of block working north of Peterborough had been connected together and the system was fully operational from London to Shaftholme and Askern Junctions north of Doncaster.

The rush to complete the block system along the main line had meant that, within a few months, it was obvious that some of the block sections were too long and were delaying traffic. As early as November 1871, Johnson had had to admit that additional signalboxes were needed between Tallington and Grantham, and at the end of April 1872, after he submitted estimates for eight new structures, the General Manager agreed to the expenditure of £2,000 '...to put in some intermediate Block Stations to perfect the Telegraph Block Working system between London and Doncaster and avoid unnecessary delay to trains...' The provision of extra layby sidings and slow roads was also found to be necessary, an early example being the additional up line between Potters Bar and a place called Bell Bar, where a new signalbox was brought into use at the very end of 1872 (*Picture 12*).

The problems caused by the miscalculation as to how many signalboxes would be needed, must have been serious, because Grinling felt it necessary to refer to it in his *History*, although it was to preface the statement that by the end of 1873 he thought the GNR '...was probably better equipped [with 'block stations'] than any other British railway company at the same date.' Nevertheless, the need for additional lines for goods trains continued to concern operational staff and in May 1875 Henry Oakley made an impassioned plea for extra slow lines between London and Peterborough, listing the delays to trains along with the number of goods trains that had to be constantly side-tracked to allow expresses to pass. It was at this time that Johnson drew up plans for interlaced goods lines through the five double track tunnels between Potters Bar and Wood Green, a response to traffic congestion that was not put into practice.

Block Working in the Yorkshire and Lincolnshire Districts: 1865-76

Because the GNR's route mileage in the West Riding was very small compared with that of the main line or lines in Lincolnshire, expenditure on the block system was not as heavy a burden on the company, and on 17 July 1865 it was approved by the Board for the following lines:

Wakefield and Leeds	10.75 miles
Leeds and Bradford	8.75 miles
Ardsley and Laister Dyke	10.25 miles
Laister Dyke and Bowling	2.0 miles
Wrenthorpe and Batley	6.75 miles
Batley and Adwalton	3.25 miles

The cost was estimated at £25/£26 per mile, 12 intermediate signal stations were to be built for £40 each, and the total expenditure was calculated to be £1,735. Interestingly, the Electric Telegraph Co, who were to provide the electrical equipment, recommended the use of single needle rather than double needle block instruments, and significantly it was recorded in the official GNR reports that these would be operated by the signalmen. The existing telegraph instruments located in the booking offices had allegedly '...not been used for years'.

There was then a lull in activity in Yorkshire until the beginning of the 1870s. During March 1871 new signal huts were erected at Bentley, Sandal and Hemsworth, so that the block system could be extended on the West Riding Railway, and that same month, Johnson reported that on the Gildersome Branch the block telegraph was almost complete '...and the required Locking Apparatus is being made in our own shops.' At the beginning of July 1872 Cockshott noted that between Drightlington Junction and Batley the 'In and Out' system was still in use, and recommended that '...this be superseded by the modern block system of working, so that the whole of our Yorkshire system, excepting the

Ossett Branch Single Line, may be worked on the modern and positive block.' The Traffic Committee of 15 July 1872 consented to this and the provision of new signalboxes at Howden Clough and Upper Batley — estimated cost £388.

Records for the Lincolnshire District are not as comprehensive as for the main line or Yorkshire District but it appears that block working and interlocking were not as advanced as elsewhere. According to the GNR's report of June 1869 referred to earlier, there was no line in Lincolnshire protected by the block system at that date, although there is an undated addition to that document implying that within months of the report, Lincoln station between Pelham Street Junction to the east and High Street level crossing to the west, had become a block section. In the same report, signalboxes (though certainly not the substantial structures with decorative barge boards of the next decade) were noted at St James Deeping, Spalding Junction, March, Murrow, Algarkirk, Boston Sleaford Junction, Boston Sluice Gates Crossing, Boston East Lincolnshire Junction, Firsby, Grimsby GN Junction, Dogdyke, Bardney, Lincoln Pelham Street, Lincoln High Street, Lincoln Holmes Junction, Sykes Junction, Gainsborough, Haxey and Bourne. To this total of 19, the GNR calculated that it would have to add another 53 if block working was to be introduced over every line in the county, with a further 15 on the Lynn and Bourne Joint Lines for which the GNR would bear 50% of the initial expenditure.

Attention then turned to the main line, and it was not until the summer of 1874 that block working on the Loop line was in hand, with resignalling being carried out at Gainsborough, Lea, Stow Park, Lincoln, Algarkirk, Surfleet *(Picture 13)*, Littleworth, St James Deeping and Peakirk station, and new block stations going up at Lucks Bridge, Pinchbeck, Gosberton, Longwood and Antons Gowt.

Interlocking: 1866-76

As noted in the introduction to this chapter, the GNR first began to take interlocking at junctions

seriously in the mid-1860s. In 1864 interlocking had been specifically mentioned in plans to enlarge Wood Green station and provide additional lines there but this was not achieved until 1870. The earliest unambiguous reference to an interlocked lever frame was for an installation at Peterborough. In October 1866 Stevens & Sons quoted a price of £130 for providing: '1 Patent locking lever apparatus fitted with the requisite levers to work 8 sets of points and 11 signal arms with all the necessary lockbars, etc to prevent cross signals' at Westwood Junction, Peterborough. For the next four years, the firm supplied and installed most of the 'locking apparatus' on the GNR. When the Board of Trade inspected Sykes Junction on the line between Lincoln and Gainsborough, along with the new connection from the latter to Doncaster (Black Carr Junction) in June 1867, Hutchinson of the Railway Inspectorate noted that '...the signal arrangements at these junctions are all of a complete character, put up by Stevens & Sons'.

Table 4. Estimates for signal huts, locking apparatus and signals, April 1867

Grantham Junction
Signal hut	£200
Locking frame with 15 levers (seven point levers, four junction signal levers, four distant signal levers)	£150

Barkston Junction
Signal Hut	£200
Locking frame with 12 levers	£120

Midland Crossing, Newark
Signal hut	£130
Locking frame with eight levers (to work four station signals and four distant signals)	£80

At Pelham Street Junction, Lincoln, the interlocking installed at the beginning of 1867 to control the junction with the new Honington Junction (Grantham) line and the existing link between the MS&LR and MR which crossed the GNR on the level there was the most complex to date on the GNR. Significantly, it appears not to have been made by Stevens & Sons. A description which appeared in the *Lincoln & Stamford Mercury* is worth quoting in full:

'The machinery is very elaborate and complete and embodies several new and ingenious ideas, the invention of Mr Brown, one of the Signal Inspectors of the GN line. One important improvement is that the points are worked before the signal is given and another that the working of one set of points simultaneously locks all the other points, so that a hostile train cannot approach. The machinery also works a small red disc, which rises out of the box at the foot of some signals, for the purpose of scotching an

Left (13):
Surfleet signalbox opened in the summer of 1871, apparently before the introduction of block working on the Loop line. It was a good example of a transitional signalbox design, displaying features inherited from the simple signalling huts of the 1860s with their gables parallel to the track, while anticipating the post-1871 structures with decorative barge boards on gables set at right-angles to the track. *M. A. King*

engine and it, like the points, is also worked before the signal is given. There is also a contrivance called a compensating lever by which chains are either tightened or slackened in a moment, without leaving the signal house, according as the temperature renders it necessary and which ensures the perfect working of the signals. By this a chain can be let out or taken in two feet. There are 33 levers on the upper floor of the house and underneath is the machinery: these levers work 11 sets of points, 2 scotches and 24 signals, extending to a distance of 900 yards.'

The first reference to the colour coding of signal levers on the GNR is made in Captain Tyler's Board of Trade Report following his inspection of the Spalding to March line in June 1867. On the 'junction stage' at March he asked that the signal levers should be painted red and those operating points should be black, a standard still in force today 133 years later.

In August 1867, a new signalbox with lever frame was brought into use at the north end of Seven Sisters Road station (Finsbury Park) to control the junction with the Edgware branch. According to one source the frame was made to Edwards patent of that year (Patent No 2234). At the very end of 1867 Stevens & Sons was awarded the contract to supply and fix locking apparatus at Wortley Junction and Welwyn Junction (two miles north of Hatfield where the Hertford and Dunstable branches joined the main line) for £267 and £195 respectively and then at the beginning of 1868 the firm was employed to supply and fit the 27-lever frame at Hitchin Junction (Cambridge Junction) for £250. 1868 was a busy year with new locking apparatus also brought into use at Werrington Junction, the north and south ends of Hatfield station, Welwyn Junction, Barkston Junction, Wortley East and South junctions and at Firsby junction.

The interlocking of levers in a signalbox, however, could not eradicate every mistake a signalman might make. Once signals had been pulled to all clear, the interlocking prevented him altering any points on the line controlled by those signals. But if a signal was returned to danger while a train was still passing over points, those points could be moved with disastrous results. After an accident at Edgware Junction on 16 November 1867, signalmen were reminded not to return the signal to danger before the last

vehicle of a train had cleared the points. The device which could prevent points being moved while a train was still passing over them, was the lock bar and/or the fouling bar. It is first mentioned, although not by name, by the Way & Works Committee following the accident, when it was minuted that '...a recently patented contrivance by which the points cannot be put in a different position until the whole of a train has passed is being tried at one or two Junctions on the Line'. (The first unequivocal reference to the use of facing point locks on the GNR came in 1874, when Johnson reported that Saxby & Farmer's patent lock bars were being fitted to all facing switches (points) at junctions '...with the aim they would be installed at stations as well'.)

The argument that interlocking was necessary at places other than junctions, however, still had to be impressed on the GNR (as on most other railway companies) by the Board of Trade throughout the late 1860s and into the 1870s. For example, it was not until Captain Tyler had recommended that the points at Barnet station

should be connected to the locking apparatus in the signalbox, that the Way & Works Committee meeting of 4 October 1869 agreed to carry out the work for £150. Two years later in the Railway Inspectorate's report on the single track Bourne to Sleaford line, submitted to the GNR on 21 December 1871, Col Hutchinson still had to insist on some very basic alterations in the interlocking before he would permit the line to open. The crossover road at Sleaford Junction was not interlocked with the down distant signal. At Billingborough he had to ask that: '...The south siding points when opened should lock the up starting signal. The crossover road points should be opened before the north siding signals can be given. The distant signals should interlock, and the up home signal should interlock with the down distant signal.' Various other minor alterations had to be carried out before he sanctioned opening following a re-inspection immediately after Christmas.

Stevens & Sons' monopoly of supplying lever frames to the GNR ended at the close of the

1860s. For a brief period Johnson hoped to make all frames in-house, and between 1870 and 1872 the company made at least 14 for signalboxes between Peterborough and Doncaster and on the Barnet Extension Lines *(Picture 14)*. There may have been others installed elsewhere for which records do not survive. The frames for the Barnet line were made in the GNR's London workshops, but it is not known whether those used further north on the main line were made there or at Peterborough. Most of these frames, apparently with no interlocking, worked just a few signals. The only information we have about the type of interlocking, when it was used, is contained in the Board of Trade report of 26 March 1872, made after Captain Tyler's inspection of the double line Barnet extension.

'Good signal cabins have been provided at the Finchley Junction, and at the stations of Torrington Park, Totteridge, and Barnet[3] with locking apparatus... There is one important matter which should still be corrected; and that is with reference to the *hook* locking of distant points — I am informed that the same system has been adopted here as in some previous cases, but it is an inferior system of "sure locking" compared with the more common system, in as much as, although the points are locked whilst the locking lever is in its normal position, they may be unlocked by pulling over the locking lever, and that lever may be returned to its normal position, and the levers interlocked with it be released, without the points being again locked. The signals may then be lowered, for allowing trains to pass over such points, at the same time that the points are not locked in position. To remedy this defect, a system of interlocking which acts properly in *both* ways, should be substituted at the several points in which the above *hook*-locking has been employed.'

From then on until the 1880s, when a limited number of frames were once again made in-house, the company relied almost completely on signalling contractors to manufacture and install its mechanical signalling equipment. Easterbrook & Co, Ransomes & Rapier, Saxby & Farmer and McKenzie, Clunes & Holland were all employed by the GNR in the early 1870s. The work of these

[3] Type 1a/Balderton — see Chapter 6.

firms and others patronised by the company after this date are examined in more detail in Chapter 5.

As referred to earlier, block working on the main line was operational throughout in January 1872, completed quickly using temporary huts at some locations and existing 1860s timber signalboxes. In some places the new generation of signalboxes had begun to appear *(Picture 15)* but it was only from the end of 1872 that a systematic start was made on building larger new permanent signalboxes equipped with locking frames containing more than a handful of levers (see Chapter 6). In May 1873, Johnson optimistically hoped to have all stations between London and Hitchin fully interlocked by the following month. During that year new Type 1 signalboxes (see Chapter 6) were erected at Southgate, Welwyn, Huntingdon (two boxes), Peterborough North, Essendine (two boxes), Bytham, Corby, Grantham (three boxes) and Retford South, and by the beginning of 1874, Johnson reported: 'We have in hand the resignalling of all the Stations on the South District between Hitchin and Peterborough and I hope to have the whole of this work completed by the close of June... The resignalling of Crescent Junction at Peterborough and also the North end of the passenger station, have been in hand for some months and will be completed before the end of March. In one of the boxes at this place, we shall have more than 60 levers...'

At Grantham the three new signalboxes were almost ready for use, and at Retford, '...Messrs Saxby & Farmer are fixing the signals and locking apparatus to properly command the level crossing of the two railways and I have arranged to put into hand a new signalbox with proper signals at the North end of the down platform where the MS&L line forms a junction.'

The building of new signalboxes continued apace throughout 1874 *(Picture 16)*. On 22 July Johnson reported that McKenzie & Holland was busy at Finsbury Park, work was in hand at Sandy and resignalling had been completed at Tallington, Ponton, Claypole, and Arksey. Despite this, there were still places where resignalling preceded the building of new signalboxes, as was the case at Biggleswade, Barkston Junction, Hougham, Newark, Carlton and Bawtry. At Biggleswade, for example, it was not until March 1876 that Johnson reported a start had been made on two new signalboxes there with locking apparatus supplied by Saxby & Farmer.

The resignalling of King's Cross passenger station acts as a link between this section on interlocking and the next, and is a good indication of the pace of change in the 1870s. On 17 June 1872 Johnson's plans for the London terminus were submitted to the Executive Committee and in October the Way & Works Committee was told the signalboxes were under construction and the locking apparatus being prepared. At the beginning of December 1872 completion of the installation was expected by the year end but it was not until June 1873 that all was finished and the three signalboxes fully operational. The equipment, however, remained in use for only six years. In August 1877 the second double track Copenhagen Tunnel was opened, followed six months later on 4 March 1878 by the new double track Gas Works Tunnel (Maiden Lane). As a result, King's Cross had to be resignalled again and on that occasion the work was entrusted to McKenzie & Holland. Installation of the signals and interlocking became a protracted affair and the West signalbox was not brought into use until 3 March 1879, followed shortly afterwards by the new East Box *(Picture 17)*.

Between 1 July 1870 and 31 December 1876, the GNR had spent £277,733 on the block system and interlocking. Fortunately, considering this substantial outlay, the company had had two exceptionally prosperous years in 1872 and 1873 and, to put the above expenditure into perspective, gross receipts in those two years had increased firstly by £180,000 and then by a record £200,000. In 1873 the GNR was able to pay its highest ever dividend to shareholders, and in Grinling's words, that year marked the 'zenith of the Company's prosperity'. Between 1870 and 1875, passenger numbers increased by 100%, the tonnage of merchandise by 35% and mineral tonnage by 18%, so the outlay on block working and interlocking came at a time when the company could afford it.

Below (16):
Stirling 8ft Single No 48 hauling a down express past Sandy North signalbox on 1 August 1887. The day is obviously a fine, warm, summer one, as the signalman has opened the gable end window vent. The signalbox opened in 1874 and was closed on 13 February 1927.
Bucknall Collection/Ian Allan Library

Table 5. Expenditure on signalling improvements, July 1870-December 1876

Period	Block system	Locking apparatus and resignalling of stations	Total
1.7.1870-31.12.1870	£919 10s 11d	£236 16s 6d	£1,156 7s 5d
1.1.1871-30.6.1871	£1,407 11s 2d	£2,688 11s 8d	£4,096 2s 10d
1.7.1871-31.12.1871	£1,185 5s 8d	£2,960 16s	£4,146 1s 8d
1.1.1872-30.6.1872	£1,058 5s 1d	£3,343 5s 5d	£4,401 10s 6d
1.7.1872-31.12.1872	£270 15s 7d	£2,715 8s 6d	£2,986 4s 1d
1.1.1873-30.6.1873	£784 14s 6d	£4,254 5s	£5,038 19s 6d
1.7.1873-31.12.1873	£1,672 19s 9d	£11,153 12s 1d	£12,826 11s 10d
1.1.1874-30.6.1874	£2,903 4s 5d	£37,924 15s 2d	£40,827 19s 7d
1.7.1874-31.12.1874	£1,639 19s 7d	£33,379 1s 9d	£35, 019 1s 4d
1.1.1875-30.6.1875	£2,058 17s 6d	£42,139 13s 6d	£44,198 11s
1.7.1875-31.12.1875	£1,668 6s 10d	£45,319 15s 9d	£46,988 2s 7d
1.1.1876-30.6.1876	£1,279 19s 4d	£42,027 19s 4d	£43,307 18s 8d
1.7.1876-31.12.1876	£1,867 11s 7d	£30,872 5s 11d	£32,739 17s 6d
Total			**£277,733 4s 5d**

The changes on the main line in this short period were revolutionary. In 1869 there were a little over 64 route miles of line protected by the absolute block system; by the end of 1876 the total was almost 350 route miles. Between the introduction of a new generation of fully interlocked signalboxes in 1871 (Type 1s — see Chapter 6) and 1876, almost 230 new signalboxes had been erected all over the system.

Block Working and Interlocking: 1877-89

By the mid-1870s, the Board of Trade would not allow any new double-track line to open without the block system and interlocking and consequently any new GNR line in this period was equipped from the outset with the new generation of signalboxes. On existing branch lines the upgrading of the signalling could take longer. In 1877 Johnson estimated that the annual wages bill for staff involved in signal maintenance was just under £70,000, and he reported that to complete block working and interlocking on all parts of the GNR would cost a further £126,571. That year more was spent on extending the block system than ever before — £4,866 13s 10d — and with interlocking and the resignalling of stations, the expenditure in 1877 totalled £51,069 19s 11d.

Another improvement in the post-1876 period, which became an important ancillary to the operation of the block system, was the extension of single needle 'speaking' or 'conversing' telegraph instruments to almost all signalboxes on the GNR. One of the contributory factors in the Abbotts Ripton accident of 1876 was the inability of the signalman at Holme to contact his colleagues at Conington or Wood Walton, neither having 'speaking' instruments. In the first estimates for completing the block system along the main line in 1870, compared with 244 block instruments required, Johnson asked for only three 'speaking' instruments. Just how many there were in use by the time of the Abbotts Ripton accident is not known but in October that year the Traffic Committee approved the expenditure of £3,013 on installing them on the main and loop line, along the Nottingham Branch and in the West Riding. In 1870 each instrument cost £10, so the GNR in 1876 must have expected to be able to purchase and install between 250 and 300 (Picture 18).

Speaking telegraph instruments were connected together into discrete circuits, with a number of signalboxes (originally passenger stations) acting as centres where messages were transferred between circuits. In 1873 the telegraph circuits on the main line were apparently still for communication between stations and not signalboxes. The circuits were as follows: King's Cross to Southgate; Southgate to Welwyn; Welwyn to Hitchin; Hitchin to St Neots; St Neots to Peterborough; Peterborough to Essendine; Essendine to Grantham; Grantham to Newark; Newark to Retford; Retford to Doncaster; Doncaster to York. Once the telegraph circuits became the responsibility of the signalmen, every signalbox was allotted its own unique two-letter code, which was transmitted to attract the attention of the relevant signalman. Just a few examples will suffice to give an impression of these codes: Biggleswade South — BG; Cambridge Junction — KK; Grantham North — AB; Tuxford Junction — ZF; Retford North — YY.

The provision of so many new signalboxes within such a short period in the 1870s increased the company's expenditure on staff and it is interesting to record that as early as 1877, a significant number of these new boxes were being switched out of circuit during the night and on Sundays as an economy measure. Times of closing and reopening varied, and some signalboxes were 'switched out' during the night only on certain days of the week but nevertheless, on the London District for example, 49 signalboxes were affected. Two years later, the number of signalboxes in all but the West Riding District which closed regularly at night and/or on Sundays totalled 149, and from then on Sabbath closures became a feature of railway life.

By the end of 1880, 188 passenger stations had been interlocked, 67 remained to be resignalled, and at a further nine stations there were no points or signals. Put another way, 71% of all the GNR's passenger stations were interlocked by this date. If points over which passenger trains passed are added to the calculations, then by 1880, the percentage of interlocked connections with passenger lines was 82% compared with 85% for the LNWR, 86% for the MR, 100% for the North Staffordshire Railway (NSR) and 100% for the London, Brighton & South Coast Railway (LBSCR).

Interlocking was not finally completed on every part of the GNR until the end of the century, the final impetus being provided by the Regulation of Railways Act 1889. Considering how much had been achieved between 1870 and 1889, it is at first surprising to learn that Johnson calculated £20,653 would have to be spent on the South District (including the main line) in response to the Act. There is no one simple explanation as to why this sum was so large but the GNR was certainly committed to a number of extensive resignalling schemes at the time, most notably at New Southgate and Hatfield (see below) involving altering track layouts and the provision of eight new signalboxes, and these may have been included in the calculations. The Board of Trade gave the GNR until 20 November 1891 to comply with the Act as far as block signalling was concerned and until 20 May 1892 for interlocking and the fitting of continuous brakes to all passenger trains.

Table 7. Expenditure for the upgrading of signalling in accordance with the Regulation of Railways Act 1889

South District	£20,653
Loop Line	£9,100
East Lincolnshire Line	£2,767
Yorkshire District	£500
Telegraphs	£1,000
Total	£34,020

Of those branches operated by the GNR but owned by independent companies to which changes had be made:

Stamford Branch	£3,805
Ramsey Branch	£2,012
Horncastle Branch	£4,280
Wainfleet & Skegness Branch	£3,340
Total	£13,437

Changes of Plan

A feature of Johnson's career as the company's Engineer, as far as signalling schemes were concerned, was having to return to the GNR Board because initial plans had not delivered the required results. There were numerous occasions when signalling contractors were asked to alter work before it was completed and many examples of extra work being carried out immediately after a project had been finished. Worried about this tendency in other aspects of the company's work, a Committee on Excess of Expenditure over Estimates was formed in May

Table 6. Signalboxes closed at night and all day Sunday, 1879

London District	56	
Grantham District	41	(included stations protected by the block system, but not yet provided with fully interlocked signalboxes)
Boston District	52	(included stations protected by the block system and single lines with telegraph and staff working, but not yet provided with fully interlocked signalboxes)

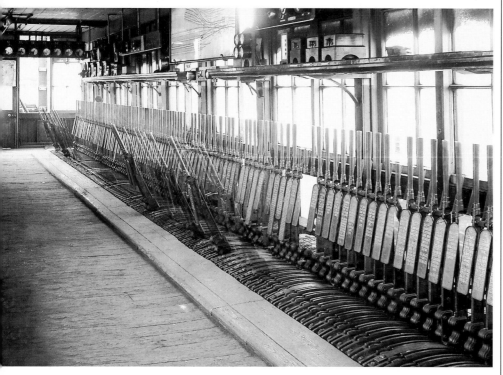

1878 and one of its first findings was that of the £480,850 excess paid to contractors building the Derbyshire & Staffordshire Extension Lines, £2,841 of which was for 'extra telegraphs'. This was a tiny proportion of the whole but the Committee continued to investigate, and in February 1879 it found that on the Bradford and Thornton Railway nine signalboxes had been erected when only six had been specified in the original contract. The outlay of £1,700 above the original schedule of prices was blamed entirely on the alterations ordered by the Board of Trade, an excuse used on many subsequent occasions.

One major rail centre that escaped being properly interlocked for many years was Spalding, ironic considering that Richard Johnson had been born there. In April 1878, although not usually one for dramatic statements, he reported: 'At the present time, nothing has been done at this station in the direction of Locking Apparatus and owing to the number of trains working in and out, some very narrow escapes of accident have occurred, and I am

therefore anxious to avoid this, and so soon as the Sidings are altered I propose to invite tenders for the resignalling of the Station.'

The timing of this announcement coincided with a period when the Great Eastern Railway (GER) had plans to expand its system by building a line from Spalding via Sleaford to Lincoln and this delayed the resignalling at Spalding. The GNR countered the GER proposals with ones of its own but eventually the two companies came to an agreement in 1879 to form a joint committee (GN&GE Joint Railway) to build a new Spalding-Lincoln link, while at the same time taking over the management of the GNR's existing routes between Lincoln and Black Carr Junction, Doncaster, and March and Spalding, and the GER's line between Huntingdon and March via St Ives (which was to be upgraded from single to double track).

Johnson was appointed as engineer for the Spalding and Lincoln line and consequently the resignalling of Spalding station was delayed again. Eventually in April 1880 he reported: 'I

Above left (17a):
Considering that during the 1870s all new GNR signalboxes were well-proportioned buildings of some architectural merit, King's Cross East and King's Cross West, shown here, looked like temporary structures. Both had to be low to allow the signalmen unrestricted views beneath Battle Bridge Road and Congreve Street bridges (the latter removed by the time this photograph was taken shortly after World War 1), but the lack of pitched roofs only made them appear more utilitarian. *Locomotive & General Railway Publishing/National Railway Museum*

Left (17b):
The operating room of King's Cross West signalbox. The original 1879 McKenzie & Holland frame of 90 levers was replaced by the same signalling contractors in 1893 with the one shown here containing 140 levers, making it the GNR's largest locking apparatus. This photograph was taken on 27 May 1931, a year and a half before the signalbox was abolished. The reason for the 'ghost' levers was their movement during the very long time exposure needed to create an image on this particular glass photographic plate. *LNER/National Railway Museum*

Above (18):
The single-needle telegraph instrument photographed in Woodhall Junction signalbox on 8 March 1969. Either side of the single needle on this particular example were brass 'sounders' which gave slightly different 'rings' when struck by the needle. This meant a signalman or telegraph 'lad' could read the incoming messages without having to watch the movement of the needle. Some instruments had tin sounders. This type of instrument, and another variation with a heavier base, was used by the GNR from at least the late 1860s and was also installed by other railway companies, including the GER and the NER. *M. A. King*

Right (19):
Hatfield No 1 signalbox photographed in August 1971. It had become No 1 in December 1920 when the signalling was rationalised but when it was brought into use in 1890/1, it was designated Hatfield No 4, controlling just the up lines at the south end of the station, standing almost opposite Hatfield No 1, which controlled down trains. Stylistically, this box was a variation of the Type 3 design (see Chapter 6), the main differences being its height and decorative barge boards. *M. A. King*

have been on the ground with Mr Cockshott, at Spalding, and seeing that the Signalling of the Station has not been altered since the line was opened in 1848, it is now important that a scheme should be prepared for your approval which will meet the requirements of the Board of Trade.'

This was not entirely true, as a signalling stage had been provided at Spalding Junction in 1866 — see Chapter 6. Over a year elapsed until in June 1881 McKenzie & Holland was awarded the contract to equip five new signalboxes and a gatebox for £4,385.

Table 8. Signalboxes at Spalding

Signalbox	Tender specification (June 1881) Levers	Board of Trade inspection details (February 1882) Levers
Spalding No 1 (March Junction)	40 (29 working and 11 spare)	40 (31 working and nine spare)
Spalding No 2 (Bourn Road Crossing gatebox)		two levers and two gate wheels*
Spalding No 3 (South)	30 (18 working and 12 spare)	30 (20 working and 10 spare)
Spalding No 4 (North)	60 (48 working and 12 spare)	60 (55 working and five spare)
Spalding No 5 (Lincoln Junction)	45 (31 working and 14 spare)	45 (33 working and 12 spare)
Spalding No 6 (Pinchbeck Road Crossing)	30 (17 working and 13 spare)	29 (18 working and 11 spare)

* operating eight gates over four lines (gates interlocked from Spalding No 1)

What makes the Spalding resignalling of particular relevance to this section of the chapter is not just the differences between the original specification and what Major Marindin inspected on behalf of the Board of Trade, but the fact that barely a month after completion Johnson and Cockshott returned to the GNR Board for permission to erect another signalbox — Hawthorne Bank — only a mile south of the station. Considering the resignalling had been such a protracted and major undertaking, and the intention must have been to make it comprehensive, it seems a surprising oversight.

The final example of changes of plan leading to increased expenditure is a very telling one, and reveals just how tolerant GNR management must have been. In May 1887 Saxby & Farmer was awarded the contract to resignal Hatfield station for £1,703 10s 2d. Almost immediately the project was postponed while a reassessment was made. Nearly two and a half years then elapsed before Johnson reported, on 11 September 1889, that instead of two signalboxes, four would be needed, and having given Saxby & Farmer the opportunity to recost the work, the price had risen to £3,299 7s 1d. This was passed by the Board, but the resignalling had barely started when Johnson was having to modify the specification again, this time citing the new requirements of the Regulation of Railways Act

1889 as the reason for the changes. The contractor added an extra £650 to its bill. Two months later in July 1890 Johnson once again returned to the Way & Works Committee to ask it to sanction an overspend of £541, and when Saxby & Farmer's work was complete just before Christmas the following year, the total paid to the firm was recorded as £5,477 8s 8d, £987 1s 7d more than the 1890 costings, and £3,773 18s 6d above the contractor's initial 1887 tender price *(Picture 19)*.

Reuse and Replacement

Apart from the section of main line between London and Hitchin, (the numbers of new signalboxes erected in London and the Home Counties and their design is discussed in Chapter 6) after 1876 the GNR tended to modify existing signalboxes rather than build anew. One example of this was the 'signalbox' at Lincoln Road level crossing on the main line just north of Tuxford. At the end of March 1897 it was reported that there was no interlocking in the box and £187 would be needed to bring it up to Board of Trade standards. The drawing prepared by the Engineer's Office in Peterborough at the end of

April that year showed a brick structure 8ft 9in by 13ft 6in, which was obviously a modified 1860s Signal & Telegraph hut. The plan was to replace the door in the gable end with a window and excavate behind this, so that an eight-lever frame could be fitted. It was not until 1938 that a proper signalbox was built to replace this 'hut'.

Crow Park signalbox probably had the distinction of being the first of the new generation of 1870s signalboxes to be extended. It had to be lengthened 2ft before it opened in 1875, so that it could accommodate its lever frame. Extending signalboxes because longer frames were needed was probably the most common form of signalbox modification. During the summer of 1885, for example, Arlesey Box was extended to accommodate a new Saxby & Farmer lever frame to control extra sidings and the new slow line between there and Cadwell, and in November 1896 it was agreed to replace the 1875 Ransomes & Rapier 'Horse-rake' frame in Sleaford Junction, Boston, with a new 70-lever McKenzie & Holland frame which required the box to be lengthened. The cost of this and alterations to permanent way was £3,572. There were obviously many other examples of this sort of modification to signalboxes, some changes being well documented, others known only by looking closely at photographs to detect straight joints of brickwork, or slightly different irregular distribution of windows.

When it came to equipment inside signalboxes, block instruments and bells had an impressively long life. Hundreds survived in use until the 1970s, having been repaired, upgraded and recycled between signalboxes, and even at the time of writing (1999) there are examples still controlling trains. The story of the block instrument is detailed in the next chapter.

The equipment which received the greatest wear and tear in a signalbox was obviously the lever frame. These were worked hardest at stations and at junctions and although we cannot be certain, it is very unlikely that any pre-1870 interlocking equipment remained in use after 1876. Despite a number of Stevens & Sons frames having been installed at important junctions only a few years previously, all had been replaced by the middle of the 1870s. Of the larger frames installed in the first years of that

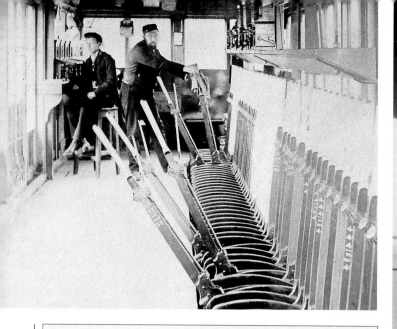

Above (20):
The 51-lever Saxby & Farmer Rocker and Gridiron frame in Louth South signalbox, photographed at the end of the 19th century. It had been brought into use in March 1887. With frames of this type the locking, not visible in this photograph, was immediately behind the levers. In common with most Saxby & Farmer frames, the descriptions of the lever functions painted on a wooden board were also positioned behind the levers, despite the GNR's preference for bolting individual rectangular description plates to each lever just below their handles. Behind signalman James Denver, the telegraph lad can be seen seated next to four single-needle telegraph instruments. *D. N. Robinson Collection*

Right (21):
This example of a McKenzie & Holland lever frame manufactured to the firm's 1873 patent (No 2034), was installed in Sykes Junction signalbox in 1885. In this July 1939 photograph, the difference in the travel of the signal and point levers is very obvious. The two reversed levers nearest the camera operated the Branch Down Advance Home (No 13) and the Branch Down Home (No 14), while No 11 worked the facing point on the down main. Only the five instruments nearest the camera on the block shelf were of GNR origin. *I. W. F. Scrimgeour/Signalling Record Society*

decade, most had a relatively short life, either because of wear or because more points and signals were brought under the control of the original signalboxes. In December 1884, for example, Saxby & Farmer was employed to replace its original Retford South lever frame, brought into use in December 1874, as it was '...worn out and not to be relied upon'. The 60-lever 1884 frame was itself replaced in April 1892 by one with 100 levers *(Picture 20)*.

The oldest surviving frames were to be found either on branch lines where traffic was light and there was no incentive to re-equip, or they were in small 'block posts', where a handful of levers operated only signals or sometimes signals and a crossing gate lock. Of the small frames installed during 1870, it is known that some of these lasted for more than 10 years. For example, in 1881 when the Board of Trade reported on stations and signalboxes that had been altered since 1870 but not inspected, Wymondley, situated south of Hitchin, still had its original frame of eight levers. Of those frames manufactured by the GNR between 1870 and 1872, an impressive few survived for a very long time — see Table 9.

The six-lever frame installed by the GNR in 1872 remained operational in Balderton signalbox south of Newark until that box was abolished on 10 July 1977. The frame is now preserved at the National Railway Museum.

Of the signalling contractors' early equipment, McKenzie & Holland's appears to have lasted better than most. Many of the firm's 1873 patent frames (Patent No 2034), manufactured and installed all over the GNR between 1875 and the middle of the 1880s, lasted a very long time *(Picture 21)*. But the commercial strength of McKenzie & Holland, as with other successful signalling contractors such as Saxby & Farmer, was its ability to be able to offer new frame designs and improved ancillary mechanical equipment when its early apparatus began to wear out. By comparison, Easterbrook & Co was not able to offer anything better when its frames became unreliable. In March 1876, barely a year and a half after installation, the frame at Tallington needed 'considerable repairs', and at Honington Junction the facing point levers had to be strengthened to maintain the integrity of the locking. In 1882 it was agreed to replace the

frames from Essendine North and South Signalboxes altogether and it is almost certain that no Easterbrook frames were in use on the GNR after 1892.

Of the other early contractors, Ransomes & Rapier was only ever able to offer its 1870 Patent frame (No 2305) but some of these proved surprisingly robust and where the requirements of the interlocking remained little altered, many survived into the 20th century, sometimes outliving their more modern successors.

Right (22):
This 25-lever frame manufactured to Richard Rapier's patent of 1870 (No 2305) was brought into use in Hubberts Bridge signalbox in 1879. It was photographed on 31 March 1956. During their lifetime these frames gained the nicknames 'horserake', 'hayrake' or 'mowing machines' for obvious reasons. This photograph is also useful in showing how the levers were arranged in the majority of GNR frames which controlled simple track layouts on stretches of double track. If there were crossing gates locked from the signalbox, they were controlled by the levers at the end of the frame nearest the crossing, in this case, nearest the camera. The up and down signals were worked by the levers at opposite ends of the frame, and in the centre were the point and ground disc signal levers.
I. W. F. Scrimgeour/Signalling Record Society

Table 9. Locking frames manufactured 1870-2 which survived more than 50 years

Signalbox	Opened	Levers in frame	Date frame replaced
Westborough	8.4.1872	6	4.10.1942
Egmanton	17.11.1871	6	14.12.1941
Scrooby	1.1.1872	6	17.2.1924
Pipers Wood	1.1.1872	6	22.2.1925
Totteridge	1.4.1872	?	1926

Table 10. Long-lived Ransomes & Rapier frames

Signalbox	Date brought into use	No of levers	Date removed
Grantham, Sleaford & Boston branch			
Wilsford	1 December 1880	10	July 1966
Rauceby	1880	20	May 1975
Hubberts Bridge*	1879	25	January 1961
Eastern Loop line — Peterborough to Doncaster			
Algarkirk	1875	30	c1951
Langrick	February 1876	25	June 1963
Dogdyke	October 1878	30	June 1963
Tattershall	1876	30	June 1963
Woodhall Junction	1877	50	1949
Stixwould	1877	25	August 1957
Southrey	1878	25	1960-4
Washingborough station	1874	15	December 1940
East Lincolnshire Railway			
Maud Foster	September 1877	10	1945

[*Picture 22]

As with its block instruments, the GNR also recycled whole and parts of lever frames. In 1881, for example, the frame removed from Grantham North signalbox was reused at Caythorpe, the frame from there being fixed at Harmston. In 1885, Saxby & Farmer was asked to quote for making up a lever frame for Grantham South, utilising parts of the existing 1874 frame which were still in 'good order' and others which had been salvaged from frames installed by the firm at Retford South and Grantham Yard signalboxes in the same year.

Another extreme example of this practice occurred when the new lines and sidings between Hornsey and Finsbury Park were almost complete and the company was inviting tenders for the signalling work. The successful firm was McKenzie & Holland, and the information in the following table has been extracted from the tender document dated 26 April 1887.

In-house Lever Frames and the Attempt to Standardise after 1889

At the end of the 1880s the GNR once again started limited in-house production of lever frames for reasons that are not recorded in any official GNR records. One compelling consideration may have been the requirement to complete interlocking imposed on the company by the 1889 Regulation of Railways Act. Manufacture seems to have been confined to the Boston District and approximately 30 lever frames were made from the end of the 1880s to about 1904. The frames (known as the 'East Lincs design' by the 1920s) had simple tappet locking and shared many features of Saxby & Farmer's Rocker frames without the rockers *(Picture 23)*.

A variant of this frame design also seems to have made its appearance in the 1880s and stayed in production until World War 1. It may have been the design referred to in 1920s lever frame lists as 'GNR Tappet 4' *(Picture 24)*. The last GNR attempt at standardisation was the use of what has become known as the 'GN Duplex' frame. It was derived directly from a Saxby & Farmer frame of 1905 and differed only in having curved cylindrical section catch handles *(Picture 25)*. The GNR did not make the frame in-house but it was manufactured for the company by a number of signalling contractors between about 1909 and the Grouping, and continued to be installed until the late 1920s.

Table 11. Signalling work Finsbury Park, Harringay & Hornsey, 1887

Signalbox	Details
Finsbury Park No 5	Additional 16 levers to be taken from frame in No 6 box, rearrangement of existing 32 levers, and subsequent relocking — £66.
Finsbury Park No 6	36 levers to be supplied by the GNR for the contractor to fix and relock — £33 6s.
Harringay Down	15 levers to be supplied by the GNR for the contractor to fix and relock — £13 17s 6d.
Harringay Up	35 levers to be taken out of existing box and refitted into new signalbox and relocked — £34 2s 6d.
Hornsey South Down Sidings	16 levers to be supplied by the GNR for the contractor to fix and relock — £14 16s.
Hornsey Up	Additional six levers taken from the Finsbury Park No 6 frame, rearrangement of the existing 30 levers, and subsequent relocking — £49 10s.
Hornsey Down	33 levers to be supplied by the GNR for the contractor to fix and relock — £24 15s.
Total	Parts and labour — £3,126 10s 11d.

Table 12. Comparable prices for supplying and fitting fully interlocked 40-lever frame 1900	
Railway Signal Co	£155
McKenzie & Holland	£163 10s
Evans O'Donnell	£164
J. F. Pease & Co Ltd	£166
Saxby & Farmer	£167 10s

Above left (24):
The 12-lever 'GN Tappet' frame photographed inside Botany Bay signalbox on 15 October 1975. The engraved 'traffolite' description plates or lever 'leads', were LNER and BR additions and BR was responsible for cutting the tops off the three levers visible which operated colour-light signals, and the release for the 'continental-style' lifting barriers which had replaced the timber level crossing gates a few years previously. *BR(ER)*

Above (25):
The south end of the 100-lever frame in Pelham Street signalbox, Lincoln, photographed on 1 April 1956. This particular frame (an example of what the Signalling Study Group christened the 'GN Duplex') was manufactured for the GNR by Tyer & Co and was brought into use on 20 July 1918. The white stirrup handles just above the quadrant plates were added by the LNER to operate the emergency detonator placers.
I. W. F. Scrimgeour/Signalling Record Society

Track Circuiting

The first contemporary reference to the use of track circuiting on the GNR appeared in a paper presented to the Institution of Electrical Engineers on 28 January 1897 by F. T. Hollins, the GER's Signal Engineer. In that paper he mentioned a novel development at King's Cross where the rails were used as electrical conductors and '...any engine with its train occupying the line shall be fully protected by the signals, and such signals shall not be capable of being lowered until the line is clear.' Unfortunately, he did not record how long the installation had been in place and there appears to be no direct reference to it in the GNR's official records, so the oft repeated statement that the GNR installed its first track circuit in 1893/4 cannot be substantiated.

In the next few years, GNR records became a little more forthcoming on the subject, and the terminology which emerged to describe what was happening at the time was 'insulation' or 'insulated rails'. The first direct reference was in April 1900, when the Traffic Committee minuted the following: 'Read General Manager's report dated April recommending the provision of electrical communication between Nos 4 & 5 arrival lines at King's Cross Station and East Signal Box, in order that signalmen may see by an indicator when those lines are occupied at an estimated cost of £286. It is also suggested that there should be an insulation of the Down Goods Road...'

The next record appeared in June 1902, when the Traffic Committee recommended installing insulated rails and electric fouling bars in the three local line platform lines at the London terminus for £450. After this, insulated rails began to feature regularly in the Traffic Committee meeting minutes. For example, No 2 Down Main and the Down Slow were insulated for a distance of 200 yards from the south end of Gas Works Tunnel early in 1903. The first use of the term 'track circuiting' rather than 'insulated rails' occurred in the minutes of the Traffic Committee for 6 January 1916.

Table 13. Insulated rails/track circuiting, 1912-18

Location	Date Recommended	Cost
Hitchin Yard, down slow	18 April 1912	?
Swineshead, up and down main	6 January 1916	£86
Heckington, up and down main	6 January 1916	£77
Shepreth, down main	6 January 1916	£112
Royston, down main	6 January 1916	£59
Honington, down Boston and down Lincoln lines	6 January 1916	£97
Belle Isle and Copenhagen Junction, down main and down slow between these boxes	27 January 1916	£164
Belle Isle, up main and slow between home and starting signals	27 January 1916	£208
Colwick Yard, north end	3 May 1917	£178
Belle Isle	3 May 1917	£154
Allington Junction	3 January 1918	?
Copenhagen Junction and Holloway South, down main between these boxes	4 April 1918	£254
Finsbury Park No 7, down main	5 December 1918	£64
Stroud Green, up main	5 December 1918	£43
East Finchley, up main	5 December 1918	£90
Woodside Park, up main	5 December 1918	£46
Kimberley East — close signalbox and replace with ground frame and track circuiting	5 December 1918	£326

After 1918, track circuits continued to be installed in many locations *(Picture 26).*

Rationalisation During and After World War 1

After the successful conversion of the general waiting room at Netherfield station, just outside Nottingham, into a signalbox in 1909, allowing the station signalbox and Colwick West to be closed, the same procedure was carried out at Manchester Road station after that had closed to passengers in 1916. The gentlemen's waiting room became the signalbox, and the East and West boxes were closed in August that year (*Picture 27*).

During World War 1 a few signalboxes were closed, often as a temporary measure, but then never reopened. Rationalisation continued and accelerated after the war, helped by the relaxation by the Board of Trade of its requirement that mechanically worked facing points should be no more than 250 yards from the signalbox. In 1914 the distance was increased to 300 yards, and in 1925 increased again to 350 yards. At the beginning of 1920 it was agreed to close Hatfield No 1 signalbox and concentrate its work in Hatfield No 4, effecting a saving of £250

Above (26): Track circuit indicator, showing its two positions. *Author's Collection*

in wages. Transfer took place on 10 December 1920. During a late January Traffic Committee meeting it was recommended that Bottesford North and South Signalboxes should be switched out during the day. Barely three months later it was agreed to reduce the number of signalboxes

at Spalding from six to three, which it was estimated would save £1,100 annually in wages. The last closure recommended in 1920 was St Albans Junction and Table 14 lists the closures from then on.

Table 14. Signalbox closures 1921-5 (in order of closure)

Signalbox	Closed	Notes
Drayton Park	1921	Canonbury Branch.
St Albans	1.1921	
Wheathampstead	9.1921	Ground frame and staff boxes provided instead, approx cost £137, saving £187pa.
Kingthorpe	1922	Louth & Bardney Branch
Bingham East	1922	Bingham West signalbox extended and 40-lever frame (recovered from New England East in September 1920) fitted for approx £2,460, saving £300pa.
Mimms	1922	Track circuiting and trailing safety catches installed for approx £1,140, saving £661pa.
Marston	1922	Track circuiting and outer down home provided at Allington Junction, approx £268.
Cemetery Down	1922	Connecting signals to Cemetery Up box, approx £266, saving £580pa.
Belton *	14.5.1922	Track circuiting and other alterations, approx £1,145.
Shay Lane	1921-3	Between Hare Park Colliery and Sandal Junction, saving £580pa.
Upper Batley	1921-5	
Gainsborough (North)	1923	
Hampole	1924	
Harringay Up	11.1.1924	Functions taken over by Harringay Down.
Bardney South	27.2.1924	
Scrooby	17.2.1924	
Dudley Hill station	24.3.1924	Batley and Beeston Branch.
New Barnet No 2	30.3.1924	Functions taken over by Barnet North, and combined block instruments installed (see Chapter 3).
Boston High Street	11.4.1924	New signalbox opened — Boston Goods South Junction.
Bramley West	27.4.1924	
East Lincolnshire Jct	18.5.1924	
Newstead Colliery North	1.6.1924	
Weston Bank	29.6.1924	Automatic signals brought into use between Crow Park and Tuxford.
Oakleigh Park Up	12.7.1924	Oakleigh Park Down moved closer to station to take over the functions.
Keighley Goods Jct	24.8.1924	
St Dunstans East and West Junction boxes	28.9.1924	
Woodstone	2.11.1924	Between Fletton and Crescent Junction, Peterborough, abolished due to completion of the quadrupling there.
Queensbury North and South Junction boxes	7.12.1924	
Ouse	1925	Between Offord and Huntingdon.
Pipers Wood	22.2.1925	
New Southgate Nos 1, 2 and 3	21.4.1925	Existing No 4 box extended.
Keighley Yard	31.8.1925	
City Road, Bradford	7.9.1925	
West Riding Jct	8.11.1925	
St Neots North	29.11.1925	

NB: Closures continued after 1925.

* *Picture 28*

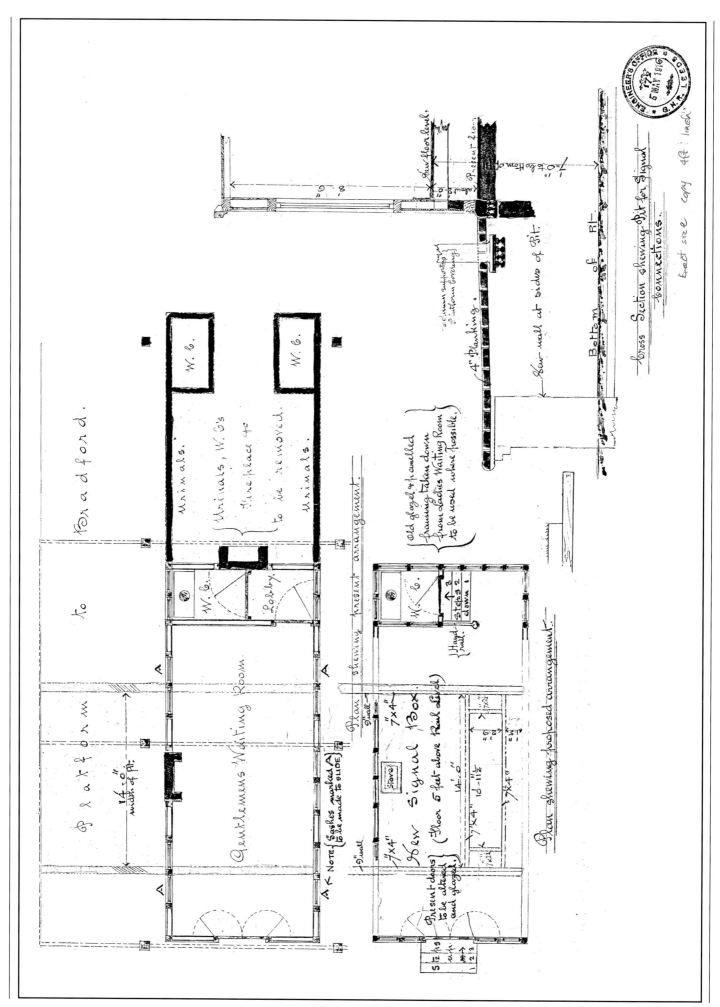

Left (27):
Official GNR drawing dated 5 May 1916, produced in the Engineer's Office at Leeds, showing the work necessary to alter the former gentlemen's waiting room at Manchester Road station into a signalbox.
John Cockcroft Collection

Right (28):
Belton signalbox was opened on 2 November 1882 to divide the long block section between Barkston South and Peascliffe signalboxes. In this Edwardian photograph, an Ivatt 4-4-0 is approaching with an up express, passing a Stevens & Sons lattice post supporting co-acting up and down home signals. Belton signalbox was closed on 14 May 1922.
Grantham Library

Chapter Three

Right (29):
Photographed shortly after it opened on 17 May 1909, this view of the operating room of Loversall Carr Junction signalbox, Doncaster, shows an early example of the 'GN Duplex' pattern lever frame manufactured and installed by McKenzie & Holland with flat-sectioned rather than cylindrical catch-handles. The photograph also illustrates the by then standard arrangement of electrical and mechanical equipment inside GNR signalboxes. From the late 1860s until the mid-1880s, the block instruments would have been fixed at the back of the signalbox, opposite the lever frame. During the 1880s, signalboxes were provided with shelves suspended over the frame, on to which the block instruments and bells were fitted. In an attempt to reduce the length of these block shelves, the mahogany cases of the block bells were reduced in width, and in some larger signalboxes, as shown in this photograph, the electromagnets and the bell were separated from the tapper. The former were then fitted into wooden cases which were mounted on a subsidiary shelf above and behind the rest of the instruments. The tapper then occupied less space between the indicating block instruments. Once dial signals had been abandoned in 1895, the GNR also reduced the size of the non-peggers, so they too took up less space on the block shelf. Six short-cased examples were in use when this photograph was taken. Nearest the camera, with 10 wires attached to it, was the block switch, allowing the instruments of the signalboxes either side of Loversall Carr to be connected directly with each other when Loversall Carr was temporarily closed.
Peterborough Museum & Art Gallery

3. Block Instruments

Terminology

The implementation of the 'block system' today is significantly different from what it was one hundred years ago and different again from what it was in the 1860s and 1870s *(Picture 29)*. It is important, therefore, to define the terminology to be used in this chapter, so there is no misunderstanding as to how GNR block signalling and the instruments used to control it evolved over time.

At the GNR's Way & Works Committee meeting on 29 September 1870, reference was made to the introduction of the 'positive block system' on the Gildersome Branch. This was just one of three possible variations of block working that had emerged by this date, all of which had subtly different meanings familiar to telegraph, electrical and other informed engineers of the day. W. E. Langdon was one of the first of these men to provide precise definitions, recording them in his book *The Application of Electricity to Railway Working*, published in 1877. For clarity I quote here from his reworked and enlarged edition of that work published 20 years later in 1897. (The current author's additions are noted in square brackets: [ ]):

(i) The **positive**, under which the [block] section is maintained blocked during the time a train is in the section, or the section is fouled by shunting operations. The indication at other times being that of *all clear* [line clear].
[The positive block system was also known as 'open' block working.]
(ii) The **affirmative**, under which the signals [and block instrument indications] are normally at *line blocked*, and are, on request, when the section is free, placed at *all clear* [line clear] for the admission of a train. A system which requires that before a train is sent forward, permission to do so shall be asked of the station [signalbox] in advance.
[The affirmative block system would more commonly be described today as 'closed' block working.]
[NB Both positive and affirmative were/are forms of 'absolute' block working, only one train going in the same direction being allowed into a block or section at any one time.]
(iii) The **permissive** system, under which two or more trains travelling in the same direction are allowed within the same section at the same time; the second or following trains being cautioned as they pass the signal box that there is a train within the section in advance of them.'

Of course, permissive block working could also be both 'positive' or 'affirmative', although Langdon himself did not combine these descriptions.

It is also useful to remind readers of the following definitions:

in advance of: from a signalman's point of view, used to describe any line on which a train was travelling away from him; when used in reference to a signal, the section of track beyond a signal (that section usually controlled by that signal).

in rear of: from a signalman's point of view, used to describe any line on which a train was approaching him; when used in reference to a signal, the section of track in front of a signal (on the 'approach side').

The Electric Telegraph

As the final section of the GNR's main line was nearing completion in 1852 (the 'Towns line' between Peterborough and Retford), the Electric Telegraph Co was bringing the telegraph into use, C. H. Grinling noting in his company history that it was electrical instrument makers Reid Brothers of London who installed the six wires between London and Peterborough. The circuit was complete to Doncaster in March 1852 (not 1851 as stated by the present author in his *Illustrated History of Signalling*, Ian Allan, 1997, p16).

The type of electric telegraph instrument operated at this date is not recorded, although as Cooke & Wheatstone's double needle electric telegraph instruments had been used by a number of progressive railway companies such as the LSWR during the 1840s, the GNR might have adopted this type of instrument. [4]

The First Block Instruments (Twin Needle)

In the first few months of 1854 the LNWR decided to work its double track main line between London Euston and Rugby by the positive block system, operated permissively, and each signal station was to be equipped with four double-needle instruments for the exclusive use of block working. One instrument gave indications for down trains, the other for trains travelling in the up direction. With hindsight this system set some of the standards for later block working, the needles of the instruments being capable of pointing to, and maintaining, three indications lettered on to the dials of the needle units — Line Clear, Train on Line, and Line Blocked. Installation of the new instruments began in 1855.

Whether by coincidence or because he had heard about the LNWR decision to adopt block working with double-needle instruments, Seymour Clarke the GNR's General Manager persuaded his Directors to sanction expenditure on similar instruments for block working between London King's Cross and Hatfield in February 1854. This was done and, two years later, the block system was extended northwards to Hitchin.

Unlike the LNWR, however, the GNR adopted its own unique method of block regulation. It chose to transmit transitory coded messages, and instead of allocating separate needles for up and down trains, the left-hand needles were used to signal passenger trains, while the right-hand ones were used for goods and mineral trains *(Picture 30)*.

For the next few years this absolute block system appears to have worked well but after February 1858, when Midland Railway trains began to run to London from Hitchin, the finite capacity of the system began to cause delays. At

[4] *It is known that the GNR had a pair of Wheatstone's ABC electric telegraph instruments in use between King's Cross passenger and goods stations from about 1853 until October 1873. By then they were described as 'completely worn out' and prone to 'getting out of order'.*

Below (30):
The dial of the GNR's twin-needle block instrument. Engraving taken from *W. H. Preece's paper 'On Railway Telegraphs & the Application of Electricity to the Signalling & Working of Trains'*, 1863

Right (31):
GNR Instructions for Signalling Trains by the Electric Telegraph, issued on 4 April 1864.
Courtesy Public Record Office (RAIL236/298/24)

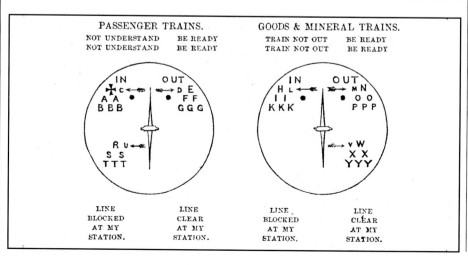

GREAT NORTHERN RAILWAY.

INSTRUCTIONS FOR SIGNALLING TRAINS

BY THE

ELECTRIC TELEGRAPH.

To Ring the Bell, it is necessary to move the left-hand needle once in either direction.

Ring the Bell to call the attention of the Signalman at the next Station, who must also ring the Bell in return to show he is in attendance.
Then Stand on the Box containing the Spring, and Telegraph in the following manner :—

No. 1.—**Passenger Train In.** Point the left-hand needle at the word "*In*," printed on the instrument.

No. 2.—**Passenger Train Out.** Point the left-hand needle at the word "*Out.*"

No. 3.—**Goods, Cattle, Mineral, Ballast Train or Empty Engine In.** Point the right-hand needle at the word "*In.*"

No. 4.—**Goods, Cattle, Mineral, Ballast Train or Empty Engine Out.** Point the right-hand needle at the word "*Out.*"

No. 5.—**Passenger Train be ready.** Point the left-hand needle twice at the words "*Be ready.*"

No. 6.—**Goods, Cattle, Mineral, Ballast Train or Empty Engine be ready.** Point the right-hand needle twice at the words "*Be ready.*"

No. 7.—**Line Blocked at my Station.** Point both needles at those words.

No. 8.—**Line Clear at my Station.** Point both needles at those words.

No. 9.—**Train Waiting.** Point the left-hand needle once to the left, and once to the right, forming the letter D.

No. 10.—**Is a Train Waiting?** Point the right-hand needle once to the left and once to the right, forming the letter M.

No. 11.—**Not Understand.** Point the left-hand needle twice at those words.

No. 12.—**No.** Point the right-hand needle four times to the left.

No. 13.—**Train not out.** Point the right-hand needle twice at those words.

In telegraphing the above signals, the needles must always be kept pointing for one-third of a minute.

None of the signals must be considered as understood until repeated by the signalman to whom they have been sent ; and if they should be repeated incorrectly, the signalman who first sent the signal must immediately shake both needles several times backwards and forwards, and again give the signal, and until it is repeated correctly.

If either signalman receive a signal which he is not sure that he understands, he must give the signal No. 11 (Not Understand), in order that the signal may be repeated more distinctly.

Between **WOODGREEN STATION** and **POTTERS' BAR STATION**.
Between **WELWYN STATION** and **KNEBWORTH SIGNAL BOX**.
Between **STOKE TUNNEL SIGNAL BOX** and **GREAT PONTON STATION**.
Between **PEASCLIFFE TUNNEL SIGNAL BOX** and **BARKSTONE JUNCTION**.

Being Stations where Tunnels intervene.

THE FOLLOWING REGULATIONS ARE RIGIDLY TO BE ADHERED TO.

On and after Monday, 4th April, beginning at 12 o'clock mid-day.—

1. The signalman must be on the look out for all trains, and as soon as a Passenger Train is in sight, if the line is clear, he will go to his signals, and when the engine has passed, he will show the Danger signal at the station and at the distant signal mast along the line on which the train, has passed ; then immediately return to his instrument, and call the attention of the signalman at the station towards which the train has gone, by ringing his bell ; and when this has been acknowledged, by the bell being rung in return, he will stand on the box containing the spring, and telegraph No. 1 (Passenger Train in), until he receives a repetition of the same signal from the signalman at the station to which he is telegraphing ; he will remain at the instrument until his bell is rung, and he receives the signal No 2 (Passenger Train out), which having repeated, he will then, *and not before*, lower the "Danger" signals, and show "All Right" along that line.

2. Goods, Cattle, Mineral, Ballast Trains, and Empty Engines, must be telegraphed in the same manner with the right-hand needle, and the same signals shown after their passing.

3. The signals No. 2 (Passenger Train out), No. 4 (Goods, &c. out), must not be given until the train has passed the station, nor until a train that is stopping has again gone forward, except in case where one train is about to shunt for another to pass, when the Signals Nos. (2 or 4) as the case may be "Train out" and (No. 7) "Line blocked at my station" must be given to the station from whence a train about to shunt has arrived, and as soon as it has stopped at the station, in order that a following train that may be waiting may come on at "Caution," as directed in clause 5, instead of waiting until the preceding train has shunted clear of the Main Line.

4. When three stations are in communication by this system of telegraphing, a signalman *after* receiving a signal from a station on one side of him that a train is "In," must at once call the attention of the signalman at the station on the other side of him, and give the signal No. 5 (Passenger Train be ready), or No. 6 (Goods, &c., be ready), as the case may be, that the station receiving such a message may be prepared for the arrival of the train.

5. When a signalman receives the signal No. 5 (Passenger Train be ready), and a stopping Passenger Train, or a Goods, Mineral, or other slow train is at or approaching the station, the clerk in charge must at once be informed, in order that he may exercise his discretion as to shunting for the following train so signalled.

6. If it be necessary to obstruct the Main Line by moving a horse-box, truck, or other vehicle on to it (*which must never be done after the receipt of the signals Nos. 1 and 3*), the signals at the station and distant mast must first show danger, and the signal No. 7 (Line blocked at my station) must previously have been sent by the signalman to the next station whence a Train could approach, who will then show the Danger Signals, and allow no approaching Train to pass from his station until the signal No. 8 (Line clear at my station) has been received without having first shown a "stop" signal at the distant signal post and a "caution" signal at the station signal post, as directed below in clause 11. The signal No. 8 (Line clear at my station) must not be given until the obstruction, of whatever nature it may be, has been entirely removed.

7. If both Lines be obstructed the signal No. 7 (Line blocked at my station) must be sent to the stations on both sides.

8. If a Train be waiting, and the signalman suppose the fact to be unknown at the other station, he can indicate it by giving the signal No. 9 (Train waiting), the answer to which will be signal No. 2 (Passenger Train out), No. 4 (Goods, &c., out), or No 13 (Train not out), as the case may be.

9. Should a signalman want to ask if a Train is waiting, he will give the signal No. 10 (Is a Train waiting?), the answer to which will be signal No. 9 (Train waiting), or signal No. 12 (No.)

10. All Trains that have to wait for a signal must stand with the last vehicle clear of both signal masts, so as to be protected by them from any Train or Engine following ; and on no account must any Train or Engine be allowed to proceed without the signalman on duty rings the starting-bell ; but if an Up and a Down Train are in the station at the same time, the signalman must leave his box, and tell the guard of the Train that should proceed that he may go on.

Between **HOLLOWAY SIGNAL BOX** and **WOODGREEN STATION**.
Between **POTTERS' BAR STATION** and **WELWYN STATION**.
Between **KNEBWORTH SIGNAL BOX** and **HITCHIN STATION**.
Between **STOKE TUNNEL SIGNAL BOX** and **ESSENDINE STATION**. (Up Line only)—

Being Stations where Tunnels do *not* intervene.

THE ABOVE REGULATIONS ARE ALSO RIGIDLY TO BE ADHERED TO, WITH THE FOLLOWING EXCEPTIONS ONLY :—

11. In the event of a train or engine approaching a station before the preceding train has been telegraphed "Out," or when the signal No. 7 (Line blocked at my station) has been received, the signalman must keep his "Danger" signals shown, and the approaching train having *pulled up at* and passed within the distant signal, the station signal must *immediately* be placed at "Caution," and the train allowed to proceed. The signalman, in the event of the approaching train being timed to stop at his station, will not, however, stop it at his distant signal, but, if the lines be clear into the station, will allow the train to enter, giving the driver a caution signal at his station semaphore. And if it is required to proceed before the signals No. 2 (Passenger Train out,) No. 4 (Goods, &c., out,) and No. 8 (Line clear at my station,) have been received, he must caution the driver by word of mouth that a "*Train is ahead,*" or that the "*Line is blocked at the next station.*"

Down Trains between Essendine and Stoke Tunnel will not be telegraphed on the Short "Circuit System," but on the Through Circuit, as per circular dated 4th April, 1864 ; and Down Trains must be signalled to stop, or allowed to pass on, in accordance with Rule 18, page 11, and Rule 22, page 13, of the General Regulations.

12. *Drivers after receiving a caution signal at one station, are prohibited from running at a higher speed than 15 miles an hour, until they receive an "All right" signal at another station, and they are to be reported by the Signalmen for any excess of the speed.*

13. Should it happen (through any accident to the wires, instrument, or other apparatus) that only one needle will move, the Signalman must give the signals Nos. 1, 2, 3, 4, 5 and 6 on that needle, and the signals No. 7 (Line blocked at my station,) and No. 8 (Line clear at my station,) by pointing the needle four times distinctly to those words on the instrument, and Signal No. 9 (Train waiting) by pointing the needle once to the left and once to the right, forming the letters D or M, and Signal No. 13 (Train not out) by moving the needle six times to the left : these signals must be repeated in the same manner by the Signalman receiving them.

14. Any defect in the instrument, bell, or apparatus, must immediately be reported to the clerk in charge, who will at once communicate with the Telegraph Inspector at King's Cross or Grantham, as the case may be, and telegraph Mr Matthews, at Peterboro', to whom a letter containing particulars must be sent by first Train.

15. No unauthorised person must be allowed to enter the Telegraph Office.

16. Any infringement of these rules will subject the offending party to instant dismissal.

Assistant Manager's Office,
King's Cross, 4th April, 1864.

WALTER LEITH, *Assistant Manager.*

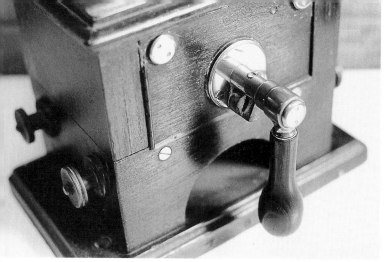

the end of 1860 the Board approved the relaxation of absolute block working between London and Hitchin except through the tunnels. The LNWR system had been permissive since it was installed but it was the inadequacies of the GNR system compared to that of the LNWR that William Henry Preece drew attention to in his paper *On Railway Telegraphs and the Application of Electricity to the Signalling and Working of Trains*. This was delivered to the Institution of Civil Engineers in January 1863 and in it he described the GNR system as inferior to the LNWR's, because the needles could not be made to point permanently to either Line Clear or Train on Line by 'pegging' the handles of the instrument. He also thought it was potentially dangerous to use the double-needle instruments for the transmission and reception of both block and other messages. It was while answering questions on this paper that Preece made the remark that the system used by the GNR was 'only understood, he thought, by themselves', a comment that has been often repeated by subsequent authors to imply that the regulations were complex and unintelligible. Like many quotes it has been, unfortunately, divorced from its context, for Preece was simply illustrating how various were the methods of block working of all the major railway companies running trains out of London at the beginning of the 1860s.

The earliest complete GNR block regulations to survive (preserved in the Public Record Office, Kew), are dated 4 April 1864 *(Picture 31)* and show quite clearly that the regulations were no more or less complex than those for transmitting 'speaking' telegraph messages. Nevertheless, Col Yolland was none too complimentary about them when reporting on an accident at Colney Hatch on 30 August 1865, which adds weight to the argument that generally the GNR system was a poor one.

Two-position ('Peg and Chain') Block Instruments

The 1864 regulations were certainly unable to prevent the GNR's most serious accident to date on 9 June 1866 in Welwyn Tunnel. The accident was described in Chapter 2, and the GNR responded immediately, Col F. H. Rich commenting on 22 June that year when reporting to the Board of Trade on the accident:

'The GNR are changing their system of telegraph. This being desirable for them to do so and to adopt instruments for working the line which shall have the means of blocking over the needles to "line clear" or "line blocked" and to have separate speaking instruments.'

The first official reference to the new single-needle instruments occurs in Cockshott's estimates for the expenditure likely to be incurred bringing a new signalbox into use just north of Grantham, submitted to the Board in October 1868. In those estimates, two bells and four block instruments are specifically mentioned. Further information about the arrangement of instruments in signalboxes can be gleaned from a request to the GNR Board in May 1870 from Richard Johnson the Company's Engineer. In his report he asked for approval for eight 'sets' of block instruments, so that block working could be brought into use between Barnby Road level crossing south of Newark and the Great North Road level crossing at Muskham. From the fact that the three signalboxes between these two locations were to be provided with two 'sets' of instruments, with only one 'set' at Barnby and Muskham, it is clear that a 'set' consisted of a bell, and two single-needle 'units'. The eight 'sets' were costed at £153, ie a little over £6 per instrument.

By 1872 the elimination of the remaining twin-needle 1850s/60s instruments for controlling the absolute block system must have been complete[5] because from 1 February that year new 'Regulations for Train Signalling by Block Telegraph' were brought into use based entirely around the indications: Line Clear and Train on Line. Although these instructions are not altogether clear, they include a representation of the dial of the single needle unit and they do provide further information about the way in which these replacement instruments were operated. W. E. Langdon would have described the new regulations as 'positive' block signalling. The bells were used very simply: one beat to attract the attention of the adjacent signalman; two beats to signify 'Be Ready' (the equivalent of Train on Line); five beats for Line Blocked; and six beats for 'Stop & Examine'. Although the

[5] *Interestingly, the twin-needle instruments were retained for permissive block working for some years after they had been superseded by new single-needle versions. This is confirmed by GNR Circular No 1,586a dated 12 July 1876, 'Instructions for signalling Trains by Electric Telegraph on the Permissive Block System on the Goods and Coal Lines', which was no more than a simplification of the 'Instructions for Signalling Trains' dated 4 April 1864. Just when the last twin-needle instrument was finally withdrawn is not known but by 1890 new regulations for permissive block working were based on single-needle instruments which displayed just three indications.*

regulations do not state it overtly, it is obvious that all the two-position instruments were provided with metal pegs (attached to the instruments by short lengths of chain) so that their handles could be held over and the needles display permanent indications. As mentioned above, a signalbox controlling double track would have been provided with four such instruments. Normally, when no trains were about, all the four needles pointed to the right, to Line Clear, painted in black lettering on a white background in the top right-hand quadrant of the dial of the single-needle unit. This indication was 'pegged' by the signalman in rear of the section that was clear, which meant that in a signalbox controlling double track, two instruments had the metal pegs holding the handles to the left, while on the other two instruments the handles were vertical (or perpendicular, as stated in the 1872 regulations) with the pegs not in use.

When a train was sent forward into a clear section, the signalman dispatching the train first called the attention of his colleague (in advance) on the bell. He then unpegged the handle on his instrument, flicked the needle to the Train on Line position twice for a passenger train, three times for a goods or cattle train, four times for a mineral or ballast train or light engine, and then let the handle assume a vertical position. His colleague receiving that transmission, repeated the flicks of the needle and pegged his instrument to Train on Line. The wording Train on Line was lettered (in white?) on a red background in the top left-hand quadrant on the dial of the single-needle unit. When the train arrived and passed that signalman, he called the attention of his colleague in rear by bell, unpegged his indication, flicked the needle to the Line Clear position either twice for a passenger train, three times for a goods or cattle train, four times for a mineral or ballast train or light engine, after which his colleague repeated the flicks of the needle and then pegged his handle over to Line Clear again.

Left (34):
Two examples of the thousands of Spagnoletti patent three-position needle units used by the GNR in its block instruments from 1876 onwards. The units in this photograph differ only in the lettering of the dial, Train Entered Section being used to describe Train on Line in Absolute Block Working, and Line Occupied the terminology used in Permissive or 'Stop & Caution' Working. *Author's Collection*

Below left (35):
Detail of Radcliffe's Patent trigger mechanism. *Author's Collection*

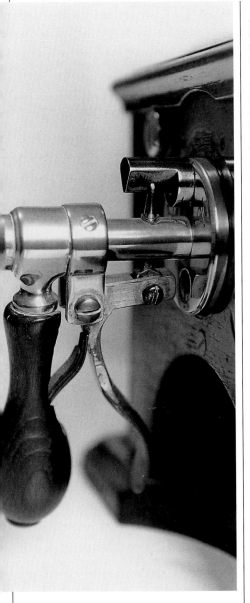

There are no contemporary photographs of these early block instruments, nor any references in the official company records as to who supplied them, so it has been important to examine carefully the surviving instruments. The late 1860s/early 1870s block telegraph instruments were almost identical physically and electrically to the standard single-needle 'speaking telegraph' instruments. Hundreds of similar instruments were supplied to the MR, MSLR and NER, but inevitably, minor differences distinguished examples used by one company from those of another. For example, the GNR favoured the block indications lettered on the single-needle unit rather than on the metal surrounding the unit, as did the MR for example. After examining hundreds of these needle units it is also obvious that the GNR specified that the small pegs (or sometimes screws) which limited the travel of the needle should be located above the pivot of the needle rather than below it, despite the fact this limited the space available for the lettering.

Of the firms which made the instruments, we know the names of only a few, because they either stamped the mahogany cases or attached brass or enamelled plates to them. Reid Brothers, 12 Wharf Road, London, continued to supply the company with both block and telegraph instruments, while the names of Harborow & Co, Circus Street, London *(Picture 33)*, and J. Foxcroft appear on the first generation of single-needle block instruments.

Three-position Block Instruments

In accordance with the 1872 block regulations, a train could be sent forward into a block section as soon as the signalman had received 'Line Clear' from his colleague in advance. The Board of Trade report into the Abbotts Ripton accident of 21 January 1876, however, drew attention to the danger of this practice and after a driver had been unable to bring his train to a stand between the distant and home signal at Arlesey on 23 December that year, his engine crashing into the rear of a stationary train just beyond the home signal, the GNR altered its regulations.

After this date 'affirmative' block signalling was adopted, the GNR being one of the first companies to do this. Signalmen were required to 'offer' trains to their colleagues in the forward section, who would either 'accept' or 'refuse' them. With no trains about, the normal state of the block section was no longer Line Clear but Line Blocked. This new third indication — Line Blocked — was indicated when the block instrument needle was vertical. A train would only be offered forward if this indication was showing on the relevant instrument. Compared with the 1872 regulations, the signalman in advance then had control of all three indications. If he was able to accept a train from his colleague in rear, he pegged his instrument to Line Clear so that the signalman in rear could lower his signals and allow the train forward. The 'Be Ready' signal became the Train on Line signal, and on receiving this, the same signalman who had pegged Line Clear, then pegged Train on Line. When the train arrived, he sent 'Train out of Section' to his colleague in rear and unpegged his instrument, so the needle dropped by gravity to Line Blocked.

When the new General Rules & Regulations were issued on 1 June 1878, it was clearly stated:

'Trains must NOT be considered as "OUT" of section, and the signal "TRAIN OUT OF SECTION" must NOT be given to the Signal Box in rear until the last vehicle of the train with Tail Lamp attached, has passed AT LEAST A QUARTER OF A MILE BEYOND THE HOME SIGNAL CONTROLLING THE LINE ON WHICH THE TRAIN IS TRAVELLING, AND IS CONTINUING ITS JOURNEY OR HAS BEEN SHUNTED INTO A SIDING CLEAR OF THE MAIN LINE...'

It is unfortunate that this change came about as a result of the avoidable accident at Arlesey, because Johnson had drawn attention to the dangers of the existing 'positive' system two and a half years before, during the debates following Richard Rapier's paper *On the Fixed Signals of Railways* delivered to the Institution of Civil Engineers in March 1874.

Although it cannot be confirmed, it is likely that when the GNR adopted the new block regulations, the wording on the block instruments was altered from 'Train on Line' to 'Train Entered Section' on absolute instruments and to 'Line Occupied' as the permissive equivalent *(Picture 34)*.

Radcliffe's Patent Trigger Mechanism

Once the affirmative method of block working had been adopted, it meant the signalman was having to peg and unpeg his instruments more often than before. It was inevitable that a quicker way of 'pegging' over the handle of the instru-

If the reader has understood these procedures so far, it will be obvious that it was only necessary for each instrument to be capable of pegging one indication. Support for this hypothesis (because there is no written evidence to prove it) comes from the surviving instruments. The author has two examples in his collection on which the handle can only be pegged to Line Clear *(Picture 32)*. Of course, there will only be conclusive proof when instruments are found with handles that can only be pegged to Train on Line.

ments would be needed, and in 1885 the GNR's Telegraph Engineer, James Radcliffe, patented a trigger mechanism (Patent No 14,954) to achieve this. The arrangement meant the signalman needed only one hand to change the indications of his pegging single-needle instru-ment and the railway company began to use instruments fitted with the new device *(Picture 35)*.

Radcliffe's Patent trigger was specified for all new pegging instruments made for the GNR[6] but there is evidence to show that the new mechanism was also fitted to older 'peg & chain' instruments, perhaps in the company's own telegraph workshops at Retford. To give more room for the signalman's hand grasping the drop handle and the trigger behind it, the instrument cases were also modified, with a larger semicircular cut-out in both the front of the case and in the base. The number of the instrument continued to be impressed on the front of the latter, the same number being stamped on the trigger mechanism.

Block Shelves and Short Case Non-peggers

The last two decades of the 19th century witnessed the final changes to block working, the type of block instruments used and their location inside the signalbox. By 1900 the operation of the block system had reached its final form and the interiors of GNR signalboxes, as well as the signals and points they operated, were to remain virtually unaltered for another 70 years (and beyond).

[6] *One surviving instrument is fitted with a small circular plate reading: 'Telegraph Works, Helsby, nr Warrington'.*

One of the first changes was the installation of shelves suspended over the lever frames, on to which the block instruments and any signal repeaters were fitted. Signalboxes built from the mid-1880s onwards had 'block shelves' fitted as standard and gradually older boxes, in which the instruments were located on the top of the battery cupboards at the back of the structure, were modified as well *(Picture 36)*. For example, in November 1888 an official report mentioned that new instrument shelves were to be fitted in Spital Junction Cabin, as well as in the 'B', 'C' and Frenchgate signalboxes at Doncaster. Such reports were typical of this period.

An interesting feature which may have been connected with the increasing use of block shelves, although it may have stretched back to the 1870s, was the painting of these and the instruments black. From the block shelves that survive there can be no doubt that they were painted black but there is also evidence from surviving instruments to show that they too were painted with the same mixture *(Picture 37)*.

Unlike the shelves, the mahogany cases of instruments were French polished and over the years much of the paint covering this finish wore off as the signalmen conscientiously metal-polished the brass fittings. Nevertheless, particularly on the sides, back and top of the instruments, the black paint remained, giving many instruments a very pleasing 'antique' finish. As instruments were returned for refurbishment by later S&T staff, this black finish was removed, and unfortunately many instruments which retained vestiges of paint until their useful lives were over, had it cleaned off by late 20th century railwayana collectors mistaking it as accumulated grime.

Another change in block instrument design in this period was the fitting of the electrical terminals inside the cases instead of externally. The first double and single-needle instruments had the battery connections (Z and Y), the line (B) and the earth (A) connections on the sides of the case. Wires could be dislodged by accident and there was always the possibility of signalmen

Table 15 . GNR dial signals in force from 1 December 1884	
Is Line Clear	
Signal correctly repeated	one beat of needle to right
Signal incorrectly repeated	one beat of needle to left
Train on Line	
Passenger, special fish, or meat train running in passenger train time	two beats of needle to left
Express goods or cattle train	three beats of needle to left
Express fish train or light engine	four beats of needle to left
Mineral, or ballast train stopping at chief stations only	five beats of needle to left
Goods, mineral, or ballast train stopping at intermediate stations	six beats of needle to left
Passenger train assisted by engine at rear	nine beats of needle to left
Goods, cattle, mineral, or ballast train assisted by engine at rear	11 beats of needle to left
Permissive Codes	
Stop and caution	seven beats of needle to left
Train out of Section	
All trains	two beats of needle to right

Top left (37):
A GNR non-pegger with its original black paint finish. This particular instrument was originally fitted with a brass plate beneath the drop handle, on which was stamped GREAT NORTHERN RAILWAY SPAGNOLETTI'S PATENT. *Author's Collection*

Top right (38):
A GNR pegging block instrument with Radcliffe's Patent trigger mechanism and inside terminals. *Author's Collection*

Far left (39):
An example of a non-pegger made from the top half of a sloping-fronted telegraph instrument, the brass bezel and glass being added during the conversion. This example had been fitted with a Spagnoletti needle unit during the LNER/BR period, with the terminology ON LINE used in place of TRAIN ENTERED SECTION. *Author's Collection*

Left (40):
An example of a non-pegger made from the top half of a vertical-fronted telegraph instrument. *Author's Collection*

Below (41):
Two examples of purpose-made, short-cased, non-pegging block instruments used by the GNR. *Author's Collection*

tampering with the connections, although there seems to be no evidence of this. All new instruments were eventually supplied with inside terminals, the wires passing through the bases into the block shelves under which the wiring was brought together *(Picture 38)*. Instruments with outside terminals, however, were never eradicated completely, as were those with pegs and chains, for example, and a large number continued in use for many years [7].

Until 1895 affirmative block working still required the signalman to reinforce his bell codes with deflections of the needle — 'dial signals'. In that year, these dial signals were officially abandoned with the adoption by all companies of the Railway Clearing House's new signalling regulations (which also reinforced the affirma-

tive method of absolute block working). The MR eventually used the drop handles of its non-pegging instruments to send routeing information between signalboxes but the GNR found no further use for them on its non-peggers. The result was a new type of non-pegger created from the upper sections of old peg & chain and 'speaking' telegraph instruments. These conversions were provided with new bases and mouldings to complement those around the top of the original instrument *(Pictures 39 and 40)*. All the bases are stamped 'GNRTELE' on the left-hand side, with a number on the right, implying the conversions were carried out by the company itself [8]. At the same time, hundreds of brand-new,

[7] *At the end of the 20th century, a non-pegger with outside terminals was still in use at Allington Junction.*

[8] *There are also a large number of conversions without the decorative mouldings between the base and the case, but none of these are marked. In the author's opinion, these are later LNER conversions.*

non-pegging instruments were also manufactured with smaller cases, half the height of standard pegging instruments, and narrower as well. In these instruments, the single-needle unit was attached to a hinged door in the back of the case (*Picture 41*). The earliest evidence for the use of these short case non-peggers appears in photographs of the interior of Loversall Carr signalbox which were taken shortly after it opened in 1909. (*Picture 29*)

Lock & Block

The names of C. E. Spagnoletti, W. Preece and William Sykes were well known in the 1870s and early 80s for their development of devices to prevent a signalman lowering his signals and allowing a train into an occupied forward section before he had received Line Clear from the signalman in advance. Spagnoletti and Preece used electrical circuitry as an addition to their block instruments; Sykes designed a completely new electro-mechanical 'lock & block' instrument. A number of other engineers also patented various devices in this period, one being James Radcliffe, Telegraph Superintendent of the GNR.

His first patent was secured in 1882 (Patent No 198) and the relevant part of the patent description was as follows:

'I am aware that there are many [lock & block] appliances... but in my improvements I ensure the locking of the signal lever by means of a vertical or nearly vertical bolt or bar, suspended from its upper end over a projecting tongue or shoe, attached to and forming part of the clip-lock of the lever. A link attached to the armature of an electro-magnet is connected with the bolt or bar. The electro-magnet is connected by the conducting wire with the block-signalling telegraph instrument at the station or signal box in advance, and in such a manner that an electric current is only passed to the electro-magnet when the block-signalling instrument is at "line clear". The electric current may be passed direct from the station in advance, or, which I find preferable, by means of any ordinary relay. The effect of the current passing through the electro-magnet is to attract its armature and thus draw the bolt or bar free from the end of the projecting tongue or shoe of the clip-lock of the lever. The signalman is then able to move his lever and lower his semaphore or other signal, or shift his points if the lever is one that works points. When the line is "blocked" at the advance station or signal box, the bolt or bar hangs down in the vertical or nearly vertical position over the end of the tongue or shoe of the clip-lock of the lever, and by its rigidity prevents the signal being moved, whatever force may be exercised by the signalman.

'The receiving portion of the "block" telegraph instrument working from the station, or signal box in advance is connected and adjusted in such a manner that only a "line clear" current from it will release the locking apparatus already described. This "line clear" current is transmitted by means of a small local battery and a "polarised" relay or other suitable arrangement.

'The whole of the "locking" apparatus is enclosed in a strong metal case and screwed down to the lever frame so that it cannot be tampered with. The signalman at the rear station is prevented from unlocking his own signal by a spring and contact point inserted in the local circuit of the lock and attached to the commu-

tator of the block signalling instrument in such a manner as to become disconnected by any motion of the latter. There is also a spring contact attached to the back of the signal lever, which disconnects the battery wire of the block signalling instrument when the lever is pulled off, so that the signal "train on line" cannot be given until the outside semaphore has been put to danger.'

Thirteen years later at the beginning of April 1895 the company's engineer reported on Blakey & O'Donnell's 'electric lock & block', which had been fitted experimentally at Finsbury Park and Crouch End stations. The firm of Evans O'Donnell was known to the GNR because it had just begun to tender for mechanical signalling jobs, although it was not until January 1898 that the firm secured its first contract with the company — see Chapter 5. Edwin Blakey, an electrical engineer, had joined forces with John Patrick O'Donnell to form the Automatic Electric Railway Signal Co Ltd, and had its 'lock & block' patent (1894, Patent No 9930) pending when the GNR trials were taking place. The patent was confirmed on 18 May 1895. As with Radcliffe's patent, the specification was based around the standard three-position, single-needle block instruments used by the GNR but with additional safeguards. In the words of the patent:

'...we employ, in addition to the ordinary electrical arrangement of the single-needle block, or other, system, electrical circuits provided with relays and having a series of contact devices adapted to be actuated by the train, the arrangement being such that a train, on entering a section, will automatically place the signal controlling that section at "danger", and the signalman at the commencement of such section will be prevented from clearing the signal until the train has passed out of the section, and he has received the "line clear" signal from the signalman in advance. The arrangement, moreover, is such that, should the signalman at the beginning of any particular section neglect to give the signal "train on line" to the next cabin, the train will automatically give this signal by actuating a suitable contact device and closing a relay which cuts out the ordinary signal batteries and brings in another and preferably a more powerful battery, and will, in any case, lock the instruments in both cabins at "train on line". The train when nearing the end of the section again unlocks the needles by operating another contact device, and, in some cases, this latter contact device may be arranged to also control one of the circuits of the next section, in place of one of the contact devices which would otherwise be employed in it.

'The semaphores or signal arms, which are under electrical control, and are all arranged so that they fall to "danger" by gravity, cannot be cleared by the signalman so long as the train remains on the particular section which each signal respectively controls.'

Further refinements to this system were made by Blakey and O'Donnell with the aid of William Robert Sykes junior, and submitted in 1895 as Patent No 1245 with R. B. Annesley. Another variation was patented in the names of Sykes and O'Donnell the same year (Patent No 2882), closely followed by another (Patent No 9159) which corrected an alarming flaw in the system. In specification No 2882, if a signalman maintained the handle of his block instrument at Line Clear, even though the train automatically

altered the indication to Train on Line as it passed through the section, once it had passed out of that section, the block instrument resumed its Line Clear position, which would have allowed that signalman to clear his signals again without the permission of the signalman in advance! As far as GNR official records are concerned, nothing further is heard of O'Donnell's 'lock & block', and apart from the General Manager being asked to look into the use of such systems on other railways following the Board of Trade report into an accident at Hornsey on 30 November 1899, it was not until the terrible Welwyn Garden City accident in 1935 that the operation of the lineside signals and the ex-GNR single-needle block instruments were properly interconnected.

'Combined' Block Instruments

Radcliffe's electrical lock and Blakey & O'Donnell's 'electric lock & block' were not extensively used, reflecting the GNR's very conservative approach to signalling. This conservatism was also apparent in its continual use of single-needle block instruments. It was only at the very end of its independent existence that the company considered using an instrument in which the pegging and non-pegging indications were combined into one wooden case. Tyer & Co had pioneered this approach in the 1860s and for many years manufactured one-wire (momentary current) and three-wire (continuous current) versions. The GNR never bought block instruments from Tyers, excepting those for operating the single line Electric Tablet System. By contrast, the LNWR had patronised that firm until the 1890s, at which point it used the standard Tyers three-wire as a basis for its own double line block instrument. The LNWR then began to manufacture its own instruments, the final form having evolved by 1900 into a neat, modern, though rather plain piece of equipment. When the GNR eventually developed its own design, it too turned to its existing equipment but the result, unlike the LNWR's instrument, was an awkward hybrid.

Radcliffe's patent trigger was replaced by a knob which operated a mechanical indicator, which could be pointed to Line Blocked, Line Clear or Train on Line. When the mechanism was pointed to the two latter indications, a circuit was completed, and the standard single-needle unit at the adjacent signalbox repeated the indications. The non-pegging indication in the 'new' instrument was the same standard single-needle unit located above the mechanical indicator. The single-stroke block bell was broken into its component parts. The tapper was fitted into the main instrument case just to the right of the mechanical indicator, while the electro-magnets were fitted into a wooden case attached to, and suspended over, the top of the instrument. The bell was suspended under this separate case (*Picture 42*).

No record can be found as to when these instruments were made but it is almost certain that they were installed in the new Spalding signalboxes when they opened in the summer of 1921. Surviving examples have the cases stamped 'GNRTELE', another indication that they were manufactured just before (and perhaps a little after) the LNER was created in 1923.

4. Semaphores and Lamps

Semaphores, 1848-76

Opening its first stretch of line in 1848, the GNR had the advantage of being able to adopt the already well-tried and tested semaphore signal, rather than having to invent its own visual signalling devices as had the first generation of main line railways in the previous decade. The GNR also decided from the outset to use semaphore signals as both 'auxiliary' or 'distant' signals and 'station signals' and was the first railway to do so. The latter, as their name implies, were located either on the station platform or very close to it, both arms, one for up trains and the other for down, usually on the same post. The arms gave the by then standard three indications — danger (arm parallel to the ground), caution (arm inclined downwards at 45 degrees), and all clear (arm out of sight in a slot in the post). The GNR's General Instructions of 1850 stated that the danger signal had to be displayed for five minutes after a train had passed (at night a red light) and followed for the next eight minutes by the caution signal (a green light at night). The 'all right' signal at night was a white light.

The indications of the station signals were repeated by additional signals positioned some distance away — 'distance' or 'distant' signals — to give drivers advanced warning. When Capt Wynne inspected the Peterborough (Werrington Junction) to Lincoln line in October 1848 for the Board of Trade, he reported that there were 'distance' signals either side of all 16 passenger stations, each signal worked by wire and placed between 400 and 600 yards from the station semaphores. As speeds increased, the distant signals became very important and barely a year after the main line was opened southwards from Peterborough to London in August 1850, the Locomotive Superintendent, A. Sturrock, was asking that on falling gradients of 1 in 200 or on curves they should be sited between 1,000 and 1,200 yards in rear of the station signals, so that from 45mph expresses could be brought to a stand if a station or junction was occupied by another train. (See Table 17 below for the siting of distant signals in 1877.)

As already mentioned, distant signals were operated by wires from the station or junction, a simple mechanical engineering solution. However, in a period when the number of railway patents was increasing, it was almost inevitable that someone should try and claim rights over this fundamental principle. At the end of 1852, a few months after the final section of main line between Peterborough and Retford was opened and every station had been provided with distant signals, a Mr W. J. Curtis of 23 Grafton Place, Euston Square, wrote to J. A. Mowatt, Secretary of the GNR, claiming that the company was using signals which infringed his patent of 1839. He asked for a royalty of £5 per signal. Joseph Cubitt, the GNR's Engineer was consulted and obviously with some annoyance replied to Mowatt in a hastily handwritten letter of 13 November, saying:

'I cannot suppose that such a claim as he [Curtis] makes can be sustained. Giving signals by the movement of an arm at some distance from the Persons operating them, is of such older date than 1839... Such signals as we have on the Line are on every or nearly every line in the Kingdom & I do not believe that Mr Curtis has been able to establish his claim against any one of them.'

Nothing further was heard from Mr Curtis and the GNR continued to erect wire-operated semaphore signals all over its system. The type of semaphore being used at this time was illustrated in a drawing (*Picture 44a*) prepared for a Board meeting on 27 February 1855 to show the design of a wooden bridge (what would later be referred to as a gantry) at the entrance to the new passenger station at Leeds. The bridge supported three posts, each with two semaphore arms. Unfortunately, only one elevation and a plan were submitted to the Board, neither of which showed any operating mechanism. Beneath each pair of arms one lamp and a spectacle with two coloured glasses was shown. At this date semaphores at junctions gave just two indications — danger and caution — and although it can only be assumed, it is possible that the lamp was designed to turn through 90 degrees to give two indications for one direction, while in either position was capable of shining its light through the spectacle to give indications for trains approaching in the opposite direction (*Pictures 44b and 44c*).

This 'three signal bridge' was probably built using the GNR's own labour, but as with most things, the company also purchased hardware and services from contractors. Being one of the first firms to make mechanical signalling equipment, Stevens & Sons was patronised by the GNR from an early date. As well as supplying signals, posts and lamps, Stevens also had the contract with the company for their maintenance. When this was renewed for the year starting 1 January 1862, labour rates were set at 8d per signal per week.

During the early 1860s Stevens & Sons had a virtual monopoly of signalling work on the GNR at a time before other contractors had become established. After gales had damaged many signal posts and arms on 27 and 28 February 1860, Walter Brydone, the company's Engineer at the time, decided to purchase a number of metal lattice (or 'trellis-work' as he described them) posts, which offered less wind resistance (*Picture 45*). The first of these posts were fixed at Peascliffe Tunnel just north of Grantham and six years later Stevens & Sons provided three 50ft examples described as 'Patent Wrought Iron Junction Signals', with candle lamps (see below) and lamp lifting apparatus, for Westwood Junction, Peterborough, at a cost of £114. When estimates for renewing the signals at the flat crossing with the MR just north of Newark were drawn up in May 1867, the four new posts were all specified as 'wrot iron' [sic], the two station signal posts each being 45ft high.

In this period, in line with the practice of other railway companies, GNR semaphore arms

Left (43):
Stirling 8ft Single No 1008, photographed accelerating past Harringay Up signalbox with a down train on 16 June 1900. Although the box had opened in 1888, the metal lattice bracket in the foreground had only recently been installed by McKenzie & Holland (note the manufacturer's cast-iron plate) to support a standard 5ft long wooden somersault semaphore arm. If the photographer had returned three years later, Harringay Down box would have appeared to occupy the space immediately behind the locomotive.
The Locomotive Club of Great Britain/Ken Nunn Collection

Top right (44a):
Elevation and plan of the proposed signal bridge at Leeds, submitted to the GNR Board on 27 February 1855. Once erected, the bridge and signals remained in use until October 1872.
Courtesy Public Record Office (RAIL236/278/8)

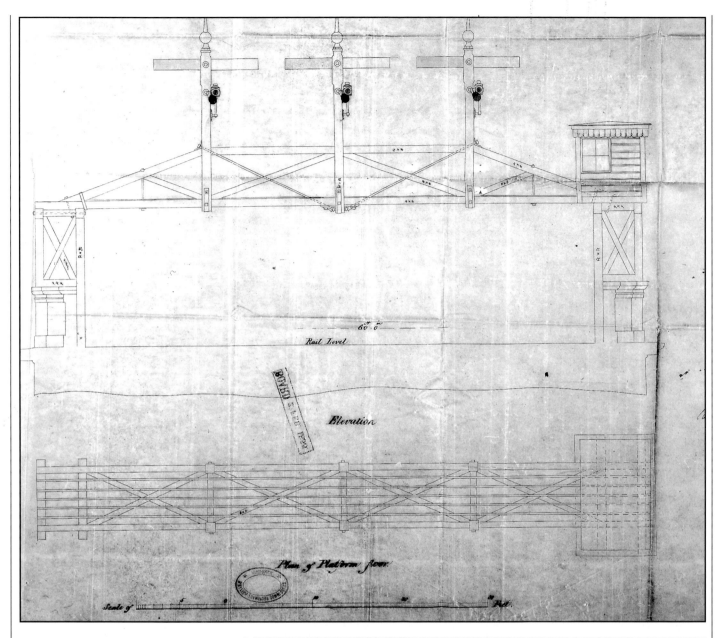

Elevation

Rail Level

Plan of Platform floor

Scale of

were almost certainly painted red with a white stripe on the side facing the driver and white with a black stripe on the reverse[9]. The only exceptions that have been discovered from official records were the semaphores brought into use on the 'junction stage' at Pelham Street crossing, Lincoln, in the summer of 1867. When Capt Tyler inspected for the Board of Trade at the end of June, he recommended that, as there were a number of semaphores, they should each display a description of which line and route they controlled. When he returned at the end of July, he reported that '...the names of the signals have...been painted black in some cases upon the semaphore arms; but they would be better seen by the engine drivers if they were cut out of the arms...' Whether or not this suggestion was carried out was not recorded and, unfortunately, no photograph has yet been discovered of this junction stage with semaphores, which must have been an impressive structure.

There are just a few photographs which show the GNR signals of the late 1860s and early 1870s on timber and lattice metal posts, both of which had finials. As with other contemporary railway companies, the timber either side of the

[9] There is no contemporary evidence for the use by the GNR of metal signal arms with perforated vertical slots.

Table 16. Estimate of cost of signals for new telegraph stations and repairs and renewals per annum, 2 September 1868

	Iron	Wood
1 x 45ft station signal fixed and complete	£36 2s 6d	£29 10s
2 x 40ft distant signals fixed and complete	£61	£50 15s
2 x pull over ratchet levers	£11 10s	
4 x 14in flat wheels and frames	£2 18s	
Repairs per annum		
3 x signals	£3 18s	£3 18s
3 x signals, painting every two years	£1 10s	£1 10s
3 x material for repairs	£3	£3
Renewals per annum to allow each signal to last 12 years	£13 9s 2d	£12 1s

slot in the all wooden examples was wider than the rest of the post (*Pictures 46 and 47*), whereas on lattice posts, there was no variation in thickness where the arm was pivoted.

By the time block working was operational along the whole of the main line in 1872, the term 'station signal' had been replaced by 'home signal', because at some locations other than on plain stretches of track, additional semaphores known as 'starting' signals had been erected to control entry into the next block section.

(Starting signals were provided at Barnet, Southgate and Wood Green at the beginning of 1869, for example.) At junctions the company soon realised that it was safer to have the arms of the home signals for each direction mounted on separate posts, and in July 1874 Richard Johnson, the GNR's Engineer, reported that this had been achieved on both the main line and branches. Elsewhere, however, home signal arms for both directions continued to be fixed on the same post and, as just one example, on the main

Above left (44b):
The majority of GNR signals throughout the company's independent existence made their indications at night by shining a light through a movable spectacle fitted with coloured glasses. Another available method was to use lamps with coloured lenses which rotated to give the appropriate indication to an approaching train. However, apart from the lamps at Three Signal Bridge Junction, Leeds, the only other evidence for their use on the GNR appears in this detail from a photograph of the trackwork at Carr signalbox, Doncaster (opened in July 1891). The four shunting semaphores visible here had no spectacles and the lamps obviously had lenses set at 90°. *Locomotive & General Railway Publishing/ National Railway Museum*

Above (44c):
Similar signals to those at Carr, Doncaster, must have been used at Wood Green, as the brass plate on this surviving lamp case with the main lenses set at 90° is clearly engraved Wood Green. *Harpenden Railway Museum*

Centre left (45):
A 60ft high Stevens & Sons metal lattice post supporting the up main starting semaphores at Oakleigh Park, photographed on 20 March 1901. The up slow line starters were fixed to a slightly shorter timber post to the left. *The Locomotive Club of Great Britain/ Ken Nunn Collection*

Left (46):
Just visible behind 2-4-0 No 281, photographed at Doncaster in the 1880s, is a wooden bracket signal with two 'dolls', both with slots in which the semaphore arms were pivoted. Immediately to the right of the locomotive's chimney, a slow line semaphore arm distinguishable by its ring can just be seen. *H. Gordon Tidey*

line at Scrooby and Sutton & Barnby Moor in Nottinghamshire the signals were not 'separated' until October 1916.

Development of the Somersault Signal

The slotted post semaphore signals common to most railway companies in the 1860s and 1870s continued to be installed by the GNR until the accident at Abbotts Ripton in 1876, which led to the design of a radically different semaphore as well as the modification of the company's comparatively new block regulations, as described in the previous chapter. Until then, signals were normally kept in the all clear position unless a train was occupying the block section, when they were maintained at danger. Once the signalman who had admitted the train into the block section was notified by his colleague in advance that the train had arrived, the signals were lowered again. Unfortunately, on the night of 21 January 1876 the slots of all the semaphore arms between Peterborough and Abbotts Ripton had filled with freezing snow, so that the arms could not be returned to danger, and as a consequence, two trains ran past clear signals into a coal train *(Picture 48)*. Barely three months later, it emerged during the inquiry into a less serious collision at Corby during a snow storm, that the semaphore arm of the up distant there had also become stuck in its slot, causing it to display an all clear indication, even though the station signal was correctly showing danger.

The Board of Trade was very critical of the GNR's traffic management after the Abbotts Ripton accident and made a number of recommendations. That signals should normally be kept at danger was a suggestion adopted almost immediately by the GNR (and other companies). But the company introduced two changes of its own to improve the semaphore signal and within a year of the two accidents the GNR had made a start in replacing its existing semaphores with signals of a completely novel and distinctive design — the 'somersault'.

There is still something of a mystery surrounding the adoption of the 'somersault' semaphore by the GNR. On 6 July 1876, only a few months after the Abbotts Ripton and Corby

accidents, the Way & Works Committee received a report from the General Manager which, because it was so short, tantalising and no further comments on the subject survive, is worth quoting in full.

'The General Manager called the attention of the Committee to the occasional failure of the Signals on the Line during severe snow storms, and proposed that the arms should be made to go up instead of down, a plan which had been tried experimentally. The Engineer explained the working of the Midland Disc Signals and those of the Great Western Company, and stated that the expense of putting "repeaters" in the Signal Boxes to enable the Signalmen to ascertain that their Signals were working properly would amount to about £25,000. Resolved that the General Manager be instructed to report on the whole question.'

Unfortunately, either that report did not survive, or it was never made.

The next piece of evidence for the new GNR semaphore is contained in a provisional patent for 'Improvements in Railway Signals', 22 September 1877, No 3569, granted to Edward French, a GNR Signal Fitter of Hitchin.

'One part of my Invention has for its object so to construct semaphore signal arms, that when in the extended, or "danger" position, the accumulation of snow or action of the wind thereon shall not have any tendency to move the signal from the "danger" into the "all right" position; and furthermore, that when moved out of the "danger" position, the signal arm shall tend to return to it. For these purposes I place the pivots on which the signal arm turns in the middle of its length, and I make the parts on each side of the pivots so that the one part shall counter balance the other part, both as regards weight and superficial area. Thus as each part presents the same area for the snow to accumulate, or for the wind to act upon, these will have no tendency to move the signal arm out of whatever position it may be placed in. Furthermore, I place the pivots of the arm vertically above the centre of gravity thereof when in the horizontal position, so that the arm will always tend to retain that position, and to return to it when inclined in either direction.'

The second, shorter, part of the patent referred to an audible signal patented by Robert Burn of

Epsom in 1874 (No 774), to which the new semaphore could be attached. The relationship between French and Burn is not known but in *The Engineer* of 22 February 1878, Burn's device was illustrated along with French's semaphore *(Picture 49)*. This is the earliest drawing of a somersault signal and significantly it showed the 'all clear' indication being made with the arm tilted upwards. Either French knew of the GNR General Manager's comments of 1876 referring to semaphores which went up instead of down and incorporated that notion into his new signal, or the General Manager when he mentioned that experiments had been carried out with such signals was referring to trials of French's somersault. French was not mentioned in the article which accompanied the drawing in *The Engineer*, but it did say that Burn's system had been 'severely tested' on both the GNR and LSWR, '...and its use is extending on both lines' — see Chapter 8. Whether it was tested in conjunction with French's semaphore was not recorded.

The only certain facts in this episode of signalling history are that the GNR did adopt the somersault signal but arranged so that the arm was pulled downwards to its vertical all clear position, and that it was used for all new work and renewals from at least 1878 onwards (it is illustrated in the GNR General Rules & Regulations book dated 1 June 1878). Considering it was installed all over the system, the company does not appear to have rewarded the inventor in any way. The patent remained provisional and there is no mention of French in Grinling's official history of the GNR (1898 and 1903), where reference to the new signal is a mere footnote [10].

The development of the somersault signal is a good example of one company's response to a bad accident which in 1876 could have occurred on any line, anywhere in the country, given the same weather conditions. The signals of the NER were just as vulnerable, yet that company continued to install semaphores pivoted in a slot in the signal post until the Grouping of 1923.

[10] *French may not have reaped any benefit from his somersault signal, but he continued to be employed by the GNR as a signal fitter and in 1886 managed to secure a full patent for an electrical point detection device, which prevented the relevant disc signal from being operated if the blades of a set of points had not been closed correctly. The circuitry also locked the relevant main line signal lever and gave an indication in the signalbox (No 4701, 1886). What, if any, financial gain he made from this is not known.*

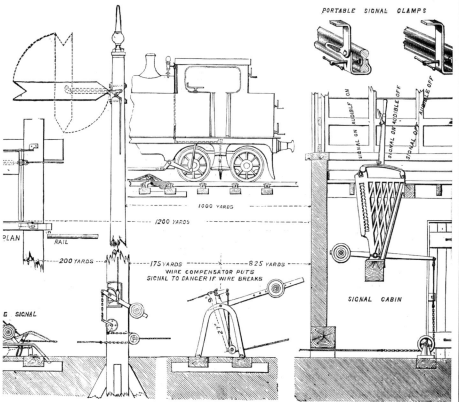

Above (48):
Without realising it, the photographer of this up train leaving Peterborough in the 1880s captured three elements directly associated with the Abbotts Ripton accident. Stirling 8ft Single No 48, hauling a down express, was the third engine involved in that accident. On the extreme right of this photograph is a Stevens & Sons metal lattice post with the original form of GNR semaphore, pivoted in a slot in the post (this particular example had been fitted with a somersault signal spectacle). To the left of the train the tall Stevens post had already been equipped with a pair of new co-acting somersault arms, the development of this design of signal being a direct result of the Abbotts Ripton accident.
Peterborough Museum & Art Gallery

Left (49):
The earliest illustration of French's somersault semaphore, reproduced along with a representation of Robert Burn's 'audible signal' in the *Engineer*, 22 February 1878.
Courtesy Birmingham Central Library

Two Aspects Instead of Three

Another puzzling aspect of the story of the somersault signal is the almost complete lack of reference to it in the GNR's records. The only mention to an alteration in the construction of the semaphore is in a report to the Way &
Works Committee from J.W. Ogilvie on 30 July 1877, when he stated that 'New pattern spectacles are being fitted to all signals'. In the author's opinion, this is not a reference to the introduction of the somersault arm but to the second of the GNR's own improvements following the Abbotts Ripton accident, namely the standardisation on just two and not three signal aspects and their reinforcement at night on main line signals by two lights — red for the
on position, and green for the all clear position. Until then, the all clear indication had been a white light and the caution signal at night a green light. At this date the semaphore arm and the spectacle were still physically separate devices, so it was possible to introduce a new spectacle for existing slot-in-the-post semaphores, and this is certainly what happened judging from the evidence of 1880s/90s photographs, which show such semaphores

with the same spectacles as those used in conjunction with somersault arms.

The abandonment of the three-aspect signal was not a direct result of the Abbotts Ripton accident but the incident obviously hastened the end of what was already an anachronism. After the extension of block working along the main line in the early 1870s, three-position semaphores remained in use. In the report of an accident at Retford in August 1873, for example, it was recorded that the up distant signal was off, but the station home signal was at caution. In the Derbyshire Extension lines signalling tender document sent to contractors at the beginning of 1875, it still specified that '...All home signals are to work to "Danger", "Caution", and "All Right" if required'. The caution indication had been used originally in time interval and then later in permissive block working, to allow a train forward into an already occupied section of line. In the rules of absolute block working this was not permitted and so the signal giving entry into a block section only needed to be capable of showing two indications, danger or all clear. How and why the GNR used the caution indication after absolute block working had been adopted is not fully understood.

The earliest references to the change from three to two-aspect signals is made in the monthly reports of the North District Engineer[11]. On 29 September 1877 he reported that new pattern spectacles had been fitted to home, starting and distant signals between Peterborough and Monkswood Signalbox, and on 31 January 1878 he stated that 'All signals between Grantham Junction and Barnby inclusive have been made to work to two positions only and the spectacles have been glazed with the new green glasses.'

By the end of February 1878 this work had been completed between Newark South and Doncaster *(Picture 50)*.

Slow Line Signals

After the Abbotts Ripton accident, the Board of Trade inquiry had chastised the GNR for trying to run goods and passenger trains together on a double track main line, and it suggested the company should provide extra lines for the exclusive use of slow moving freight trains. The company's response was to provide extra 'layby' sidings and short stretches of additional track where it was felt necessary. One of the first of these was brought into use between Cambridge Junction and Cadwell signalboxes in January 1877, and the semaphore arms controlling it were

[11] *Reports from other Districts do not survive, but it must be assumed the changes were common to all Districts.*

fitted with rings to distinguish them from signals controlling the adjacent main line. Similar rings were used by other companies for the same purpose. The practice was extended to all GNR slow and 'additional' lines from then on, while at the same time the all clear aspect was altered from white to purple, the first mention of this appearing in the company's General Rules & Regulations of 1 June 1878. The external diameter of the rings measured 30in, and the internal 21in, making them 4½in wide; interestingly those on the LNWR were of exactly the same external dimension. That company continued to use rings until the Grouping, while those on the GWR lasted for another 50 years after that. But the GNR was not so convinced of their usefulness, and when new lines were laid and considerable extensions to existing ones made in the 1880s, it was concerned about the possibility of confusion, as the designation of lines changed during the alterations. As a result, during 1887, not only was a start made on removing rings from semaphores, but the use of a purple all clear aspect was also abandoned and green substituted for the all clear indication. By the end of April that year, this had been achieved between Hatfield and Newark South, and was completed to Shaftholme Junction and throughout the West Riding (Yorkshire) District in May. A purple light was then used as the backlight in all signals, where green had been used previously. This change was completed in the North District by January 1888.

Early Somersaults

In a number of tender documents issued in the 1870s it was specified that home and starting signals should be worked by rods from the signalbox, and distant signals and ground discs by wires. Any distant signal further than 500

yards from the signalbox (which must have been the majority) had to have a wire compensator. With the ever-increasing number of signals and points, the use of rod-worked semaphores could not have survived long into the 1880s.

Until the beginning of the 20th century, all somersault arms were always mounted a few feet above the lamp and spectacle to which they applied *(Picture 51)*. Photographs of the first generation of somersault signals also show three interesting details which tended to disappear in the new century.

The first was the means provided for the lampmen and signal fitters to climb the post. Before the GNR started to use long-burning lamps in the first decade of the 20th century, lamps were taken out to signals just before nightfall and then taken in again at daybreak. 'Lifting apparatus' supplied by Stevens & Sons in 1866 has already been mentioned, and in the documentation to signalling contractors issued in the first years of the 1870s, windlasses were specified for raising and lowering lamps. How widespread their use was is not known and on most signals metal ladders were attached to the posts from ground level to the lamp and spectacle. Between the spectacle and the arm, cast-iron steps or footholds were fitted onto the post at intervals of 1ft 9in. Presumably the logic was that as the arm and its fittings had to be accessed less frequently than the lamp and spectacle, it was cheaper to provide these footholds than a full ladder. The safety of employees was viewed very much as a matter of personal care and vigilance, and consequently the GNR rarely provided a hoop at the top of ladders, and on single posts these, and platforms or landing stages, were very rare until the first decade of the 20th century. Considering the height of the majority of GNR signals, and the fact that the distance between the end of the ladder and the top of the post was often many tens of feet, few other railway companies expected so much manual dexterity and sheer courage from their signal fitters *(Picture 52)*.

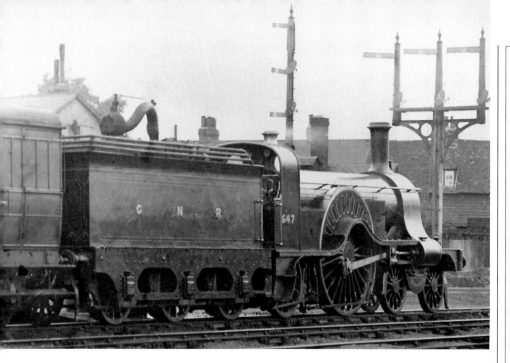

Left (51):
Another example of 'slot-in-the-post' semaphore signals that were originally erected during the resignalling of the main line in the early 1870s and then modified after 1877 by the fitting of somersault arms and two-aspect spectacles. When this photograph was taken in the 1890s, the signal post immediately above Stirling 8ft Single No 547's cab still had one miniature semaphore arm at the top pivoted within the post, with its spectacle almost in line with the next arm beneath it. In front of the engine, the three-doll signal had a variation of the cast-iron bracket shown in the previous picture, a variation which appears to have been a more common one, being also used on level crossing gates — *see Picture 117. Author's Collection*

Centre left (52):
4-4-2 No 1442 approaching Greenwood signalbox and Hadley Wood Tunnel shortly after World War 1. The cast-iron footholds on the top half of both signal posts can be seen clearly, and as with many other co-acting signals, only the bottom semaphores were provided with spectacles. Also worthy of note is the relative size of the semaphore arms. Those at the top of the posts were standard 5ft arms, while the co-acting arms beneath were 4ft examples.
Locomotive & General Railway Publishing

Below left (53):
A wonderful line-up of locomotives, railway staff and their families at the Lincolnshire junction of Firsby in the early 1880s. On the left is the local train to Spilsby, a train for Boston is in the centre and on the right is the Skegness train. Of signalling interest is the three-doll bracket immediately adjacent to the signalbox. Each signal had the spectacle and lamp mounted on the same side of the post as the arm, an arrangement not as common as that illustrated by the somersault signal on the right of this photograph with the spectacle opposite the arm. Every movable object and everybody in this photograph was obviously arranged specially for the photographer and, as a bonus for later signalling historians, just visible through the gable end windows of the signalbox are two hand lamps placed on special stands. These lamps would have been lit and put into these positions only during fog and falling snow, a requirement added to the Rules and Regulations following the Abbotts Ripton accident. *A. J. Ludlam Collection*

The second interesting feature of early somersault signals was the way the spectacle and lamp could be attached to either side of the post. Normally when a driver was approaching a signal, the spectacle and lamp were fitted on the right-hand side of the post but on a small number of signals they were fitted on the left-hand side *(Picture 53)*. There appears to be no satisfactory explanation for this alternative arrangement.

The third anomaly which can be detected by looking at photographs of early signals, is the positioning of the cast iron bracket onto which the arm was pivoted. In line with the practice of all other railway companies, the majority of GNR signals made their indications on the left-hand side of the post as seen by an approaching driver *(Picture 54)*. But in a very few cases, the arm was hung on a bracket extending on the right-hand side of the post. Unlike the spectacle castings, which could be used either way, the bracket for such signals must have been cast from a different mould.

By the end of the century, according to an official drawing prepared by the Engineer's

Office in Peterborough and dated 9 June 1899, the GNR was using three different wooden semaphore arms; distant, stop and miniature *(Picture 55)*. Of these, the first two were 10in wide by 5ft long, and the third, the miniature arm, was 6in wide by 2ft 6in long. Photographic and physical evidence, however, indicates that at least one other length of arm was in use at this time, measuring 4ft long. This appears to have been used for exits from slow, loop or platform lines onto other running lines and there is no explanation as to why it was not included on the official 1899 drawing.

Distant Signals

In pre-absolute block working days, a driver had been expected to stop at a distant in the on position, and then be permitted forward at caution, in case another train was at the home signal. To allow this, a distant signal had to be capable of being lowered while the home signal was still at danger, the distant semaphore acting almost as an 'outer' home signal. At the end of February 1878 Johnson reported that '...between Hougham and Shaftholme the levers working the home and distant signals are being made to interlock'. What this comment tells us is that from at least this time it had become standard practice to lower the distant signal only if the home signal had been pulled off, and consequently the locking on the earliest new lever frames of the 1870s was being altered so that the signalman could not physically pull over the distant signal lever until the home signal lever had been reversed.

Although this alteration meant that drivers seeing a distant in the off position then knew the home signal was all clear, and conversely if it was in the on position the line was only clear 440 yards beyond the next home signal at danger, the new General Rules & Regulations issued by the GNR on 1 June 1878 still stated that a driver had to be able to stop his train at a distant signal if he saw it in the on position, before passing it and proceeding cautiously to the home signal.

When this rule was relaxed is not known but eventually drivers were allowed to pass distant signals at danger without stopping, and to help them react correctly to what were in effect two different danger indications on distant and stop signals, the GNR began to cut a V-shaped notch out of the end of distant signal arms, probably during 1878, in line with the latest Board of Trade requirements.

Slotting

Having a distant signal arm that was physically different from a stop arm led to another alteration to the way in which semaphores were operated. Until 1878, if two signalboxes were close together, one of the boxes was not always provided with a separate distant signal arm if the home signal of the neighbouring box could be 'slotted' instead. In other words, the distant signal lever in one signalbox would not always operate a signal arm but just a slotting mechanism instead. This mechanism ensured that the arm would not drop to the all clear position until both signalmen had reversed their levers. After this date it became standard practice (in line with Board of Trade requirements) that if the distant signal of one box was likely to be close to the home or starting signal of an adjacent box, it was fixed beneath that stop signal. The slotting was then arranged so that the distant signal only

Table 17. Distance of distant signals from signalboxes 1877
Statistics for a short section of main line between Crescent Junction, Peterborough, and Grantham South have been chosen because the up line, being on a falling gradient southwards from Stoke signalbox, has always been one of the East Coast main line's race tracks and it obviously affected the positioning of signals. It is interesting to note, by the number of up line distant signals over 1,000 yards from their respective home signals, how important the GNR considered the siting of these signals was when running fast trains with no more than brakes on the engine tender and on the rear guard's van.

Crescent Junction, Peterborough	down distant	1,253yd south
Spital Junction	down distant	675yd south
	up distant	635yd north
Walton	down distant	733yd south
	up distant	699yd north
Werrington Junction	down distant	738yd south
	up distant	1,055yd north
	up loop distant	960yd north
Helpstone	down distant	985yd south
	up distant	1,039yd north
Tallington	down distant	1,029yd south
	up distant	1,210yd north
Greatford	down distant	1,018yd south
	up distant	1,099yd north
Essendine South	down distant	976yd south
	up distant	originally slotted the North box's up home and up distant signals
Essendine North	down distant	originally slotted the South box's home and distant, then from 29.4.1879 a separate arm was fitted 378yd south
	up distant	1,182yd north
Monkswood	down distant	853yd south
	up distant	1,247yd north
Bytham	down distant	1,143yd south
	up distant	1,455yd north
Creeton	down distant	1,044yd south
	up distant	1,232yd north
Swayfield	down distant	877yd south
	up distant	1,105yd north
Corby	down distant	1,135yd south
	up distant	1,023yd north
Burton	down distant	765yd south
	up distant	1,297yd north
Stoke	down distant	829yd south
	up distant	496yd north
Ponton	down distant	1,008yd south
	up distant	935yd north
Saltersford	down distant	1,264yd south
	up distant	796yd north
Grantham South	down distant	1,111yd south
	up distant	337yd north

came off if the home signal was pulled to all clear, and if the distant signal lever was put back to normal in the lever frame before the adjacent signalman had returned his home signal lever, the slotting caused both arms to return to danger simultaneously *(Pictures 56a, b and c)*. This arrangement was first mentioned in the GNR's General Rules & Regulations issued on 1 June 1878 and this form of slotting also became standard practice on all other British railway companies.

Needless to say, old practices continued and in May 1881, when the Railway Inspectorate of the Board of Trade inspected 23 GNR stations and

G.N.R. SIGNAL ARMS.

Scale, 1 inch to a foot.

DISTANT SIGNAL

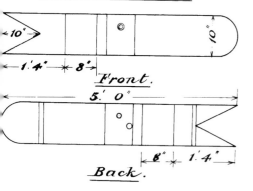

HOME & STARTING SIGNALS.

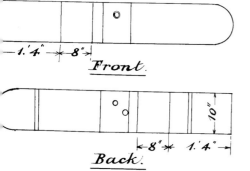

MINIATURE SIGNAL.

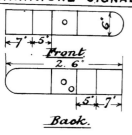

signalboxes which had escaped inspection at the time they opened in the 1870s, Major Marindin had to draw attention to arrangements at Hitchin, where, '...In the north box the down distant signals are merely indications in the Yard box — Out of door Signals should be provided.' The same was the case at Sandy and Huntingdon.

Sunday Working

Even after the Board of Trade had criticised the provision of slots instead of independent distant signals, the GNR continued to install numerous distants whose operation was controlled via slotting from two or three signalboxes if they were close together. In a number of places, the slotting between two adjacent signalboxes was so arranged that the distant signal of the box which was switched out on a Sunday could be worked by its neighbour. An early example of this was brought into use at Newark in January 1881: 'Wire in the Junction cabin to the down main distant arranged to connect with the wire to the South cabin down distant so both can be worked from the South cabin when the Junction cabin is closed.' (See Table 18, p46.)

Complexity

During the 1880s and '90s the mechanical signalling on certain parts of the GNR, particu-

larly in the London suburbs, grew in complexity. Sometimes extra signals and signalboxes were fitted into existing layouts where there were already signals and signalboxes, and sometimes comprehensive resignalling schemes accompanied extensive alterations to station layouts or yards. This inevitably led to a considerable variation of signalling practice in and between Districts. Photographs of the 1880s show there were very few signal posts which supported more than a handful of signal arms, and individual 'dolls' on brackets were often fitted with semaphores for both up and down lines to reduce the amount of timber required (*Picture 57*). By contrast, during the 1890s and into the 20th century, brackets and gantries straddling many tracks became massive structures with numerous arms, those for up and down lines almost always on their own dolls (*Pictures 58 and 59*). The company appears to have had no hard and fast rules about the distribution of semaphores on these structures. Semaphores next to each other could control diverging routes from a single route, or adjacent but separate lines, or a combination of both. The overriding criterion was to put signals on tall posts, so they could be seen by drivers from as far away as possible while travelling as quickly as possible.

As with other companies, the GNR originally used a number of arms stacked vertically at some junctions and to control entry into a fan of sidings, but long after others had abandoned the practice for other than sidings, the GNR persisted with it. There were a number of locations in the London area where this arrangement using full-

Left (56a):
Signalling contractors could supply various forms of slotting and from photographic evidence the GNR is known to have used at least two designs. This photograph shows the standard three-balance weight variety, this example fitted to the post carrying Sherwood signalbox's up starter and St Ann's Well's distant on the Nottingham Suburban Railway. Interestingly, on this signal the cranks for transferring the movement of the rods to the spectacles and the arms were mounted on the back of the post with a spindle through the post. Notice also that as the photograph was taken during the day, the lamps and their cases were not positioned behind the spectacles. *R. Tarpey Collection*

Right (56b):
The more complicated 'wire slot'. In this photograph the camera was positioned on the line on which a train was approaching the signal from the left, with both the stop and distant arms showing all clear. The mechanism with the three pulley wheels is the slotting apparatus, while to the right is the detector. The wire around the pulley furthest away from the camera is from the stop signal lever. Because this particular signal has two distant signal arms, one being a directing arm, there is a pair of pulleys on the other side of this mechanism. The wires around these are connected to the cranks operating the distant arms, while the wire attached to the frame around this pair of pulleys (connecting their pivots) is attached to the crank operating the rod to the stop signal. Because all three pulleys are attached to the same sliding bar, when the stop signal lever is pulled to all clear, it pulls all three pulleys to the left, taking the slack out of the distant signal wires while at the same time pulling the stop arm to all clear. When the signalman in advance pulls his distant signal lever to all clear, because the wire to the crank operating this arm is tensioned (as shown in this photograph), the arm is pulled to all clear. If the stop signal had not been all clear, pulling the distant signal wire would only have taken the slack out of the system. If the stop signal lever was replaced to normal in the frame before that of the distant signal, the weight of the arm and rod pulled all the pulleys to the right, returning all arms to danger by gravity. In the arrangement shown in this photograph, a detector is necessary to ensure that the points in advance, to which the directing distant applied, are properly set and the stop signal has been cleared.
Ian Allan Library

Lower right (56c):
The semaphores operated by the wire slotting described above. *Ian Allan Library*

Table 18. Sunday working of signals as recorded in the Appendix to the Book of Rules & Regulations and to the Working Timetables 1905

The wording of the signalmen's instructions for signalboxes at Biggleswade, St Neots, Huntingdon, Tallington and Essendine were basically the same:

'When Biggleswade North box is closed, the south box will work the north box up main distant signal as an outer distant. The north box signalman must, immediately before closing the box, place his up main line distant signal to danger, lock the lever in that position, adjust the wire, and take the key to the south box to enable the signalman on duty to liberate his special up main line distant signal lever, and adjust his signal, care being taken that no train is delayed while the key is being transferred. On reopening the north box the signalman must fetch the releasing key from the south box, and replace it in the socket in the north frame, care being taken to properly adjust the wire before commencing to work the signal.'

Signalbox closed	Signal	Signalbox open	Signal
Biggleswade North	up main distant	Biggleswade South	Sunday up main distant
St Neots North	up main distant	St Neots South	Sunday up main distant
Huntingdon South	up main starting	Huntingdon North	Sunday up main starting
Tallington North	up main distant	Tallington South	Sunday up main distant
	up goods distant		Sunday up goods distant
Essendine North	up main distant	Essendine South	Sunday up main distant
Bingham East	up advance (starting?)	Bingham West	the instructions in this case simply stated that the signals would be disconnected and worked from the West box when the East was closed, no procedures were mentioned
	down home		
	down distant		
Daybrook Junction	down distant	Daybrook station	'The Daybrook Junction signalman must, on going off duty, disconnect his down distant signal and connect it to the station box, and turn the electric switch, thus transferring the Daybrook Junction electric connections to the Daybrook station box.'
Eastwood South	down distant	Eastwood North	down distant — no accompanying instructions
Bardney North	up and down homes	Bardney South	no instructions
Washingborough station	up starting	Washingborough Junction	up advance (starting?) — no instructions
Nostell South Junc	down main home	Nostell station	down main starting — no instructions
Manchester Rd East	up home	Manchester Rd West	up main starting — no instructions

below the semaphore arms to which they applied but always installed in line horizontally *(Picture 62)* to try and match the practice of other railway companies, who had by then been able to combine both the arm and spectacle into one unit. The GNR continued to install new, or renew, some impressively tall posts, gantries and brackets but the lamps were almost always located immediately adjacent to the arms. Cast-iron footholds instead of ladders were no longer fitted to new signal posts and a change which can be detected from photographs is the increased use of metal lattice posts for some of the larger structures in place of timber. Naturally, in many locations old equipment conforming to old ideas remained in use or was renewed exactly as before, and in Lincolnshire signals with semaphore arms separated from spectacles and lamps continued in use until the end of the 1960s.

Instructions as to the Sighting of Signals, proposed by A. Ross in 1902

Distant Signals

These Signals should be fixed at a uniform distance of 900 yards from the Home Signal, unless the gradient is a rising one, in which case a distance of 800 yards will be sufficient. In special cases a Distant Signal may be fixed at a distance of 1,100 yards from the Home Signals, provided that a sufficient direct route of wire connections can be obtained to ensure the Signal working freely. On no account must a Distant Signal be fixed at a greater distance than 1,100 yards from the Home Signal.

Home Signals

These Signals should be seen by a Driver from the Distant Signal, and must be fixed as close to the signal-box as possible, so that a Driver, whose engine is standing at the Signal, may be verbally communicated with by the Signalman. *(Picture 63)*

Junction Signals

The same rule applies to the sighting of these Signals as for Home Signals. They must be fixed near the facing-points to which they apply, and in no case must be a greater distance than 200 yards from the facing-points, unless repeater signals or duplicate locking-bars are provided. Junction Signals for protecting a Junction in the trailing direction should be fixed so far from the fouling point as to afford as large a margin as possible for a Driver, should he accidentally draw past the Signal. Junction Signals must not in any case be placed on the same post one above the other, but a separate post must be provided for each Signal. This rule need not apply to Bay Starting or other subordinate signals; in these cases the Signals may be placed on a single post, one Signal above the other. The top Signal must then apply to the road leading off to the left hand, the second Signal to the next left hand road, and so on.

sized home signals survived into the 1950s and '60s *(Picture 60)* and at Holloway there were even two distant signals mounted in the same way, indicating the aspect of the signals from the up slow into King's Cross Goods Yard. Drivers needed to have very good route knowledge to be able to distinguish between signals.

What can also be seen in a number of old photographs, of which there is hardly any mention in the company's records, are signal wires suspended from timber posts like telegraph wires. The earliest reference to this method of connecting the levers in the signalbox to the signals occurs in January 1875, when the company was settling Saxby & Farmer's account for work at Crescent Junction, Peterborough. At this location it was recorded that 19 timber posts had been erected '...for carrying wire connections overhead containing 336ft run'. Elsewhere, the evidence is only photographic: Baldock, New Southgate, Hatfield, Grantham South, and Doncaster both north and south of the station *(Picture 61)*. At Pelham Street crossing, Lincoln, the point rodding was taken over both the road level crossing and the line to the MR station on a wrought-iron bridge.

Changes 1902-20

As detailed in Chapter 1, the creation of the post of Signal Superintendent in 1902 was an attempt to rationalise not only the variety of equipment purchased from contractors and made in-house but also the way it was installed and operated, which over the years had incorporated GNR, contractors' and Board of Trade ideas. Although there is no direct evidence other than photographic, it appears that after this date, spectacles and lamps were no longer positioned some feet

Right (57):
2-2-2 No 231 passing through Hatfield station at 2.17pm on 29 August 1889 with an up express. This was the year when the station was undergoing a major resignalling. Saxby & Farmer had secured the work in May 1887 for £1,703 10s 2d, having installed the first comprehensive interlocking in 1875/6. In September 1889, Johnson reported to the Board that four signalboxes would be required at Hatfield, and by the time the work was completed in 1890/1 the costs of the resignalling had risen to £5,477 8s 8d. It is difficult to be sure whether the signals visible in this photograph were erected during the resignalling, or whether they were earlier. Whatever the truth, the scene does show very clearly that the positioning of signal posts, semaphore arms and spectacles in the 1880s was less 'organised' than it became a decade later. *E. J. Bedford/National Railway Museum*

Centre right (58):
An official GNR Engineer's Department photograph taken in the first decade of the 20th century, of the new signal bracket and semaphores erected to control down trains at Decoy No 1, Doncaster, the signalbox visible to the left. The photographer was looking towards Decoy No 2 which controlled up trains only — a tidy arrangement compared to Hatfield in the 1880s.
Peterborough Museum & Art Gallery

Below right (59):
Another official photograph of the same date, showing a new signal gantry or signal bridge between the signalboxes of Decoy No 2 and Red Bank, Doncaster, the latter just visible in the background. All the semaphore arms are the standard 5ft long versions, with a 7ft gap between home and distant signals on the same doll. Immediately behind the post in the foreground with the stay wires, a fogman's hut has been correctly tipped up while not in use, in front of the levers operating Clayton's Patent Fog-signalling Apparatus — see Chapter 8.
Peterborough Museum & Art Gallery

Platforms Starting Signals

These must be sighted at a height of about 15ft above rail-level, and it will be sufficient if they be seen by a Driver from the Home Signal. This rule will not apply if the Starting Signal Post carries the Distant Signal of a signal-box in advance, or if the Starting Signal acts as a Home Signal for a signal-box in advance. In these cases the Signals must be sighted as Distant and Home Signals respectively.

Advance Starting Signals

These Signals should be sighted about 15ft above rail-level; they should be seen by a Driver from the Platform Starting Signal, and must not be at a greater distance from the signal-box than 440 yards. If any engine or other obstruction standing at the Advance Starting Signal cannot be clearly seen by the Signalman, the Signal must not be provided, and it will then be necessary for the Sidings in advance of the Platform Starting Signal to be worked in the block. Bay Starting and other subordinate Signals should be of a uniform height of about 15ft above rail-level.

Left (60):
This gantry of somersault arms survived World War 2 to be photographed on 1 June 1951, as 2-6-4T No 67791 pulls away from Finsbury Park with an up train from Huntingdon. Note that the gap between the stop and distant arms is the standard 7ft but the vertically stacked stop arms, because they apply to diverging routes, are positioned closer together, much as miniature arms would have been in controlling shunting movements.
P. J. Lynch

Below (61):
The Royal Train heading southwards from Doncaster behind 4-4-2 No 1449 in October 1916. The photograph was taken from Bridge Junction signalbox with Shakespeare signalbox on the right. Prominent on the left are the overhead runs of signal wires. Shakespeare box had opened on 8 June 1891 to take over the control of up trains from Bridge Junction, but was closed on 18 April 1926 when Bridge Junction once again took over responsibility for both up and down train movements at this location.
National Railway Museum

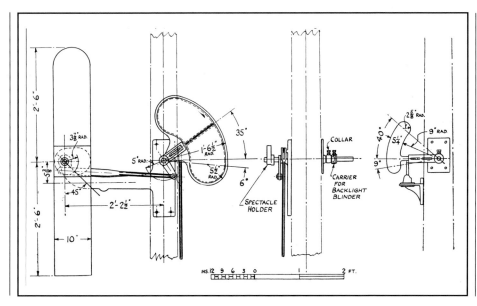

Left (62):
Elevations of a standard somersault signal with its spectacle in line with the arm.
*O. S. Nock/The Model Engineer,
13 February 1941*

Above (63):
Unlike its successor the LNER, the GNR did not use W. Sykes' illuminated banner signals to repeat the aspect of semaphores which it was not possible to see at the correct braking distant because of some obstruction. The GNR used (sparingly) instead a miniature stop semaphore arm painted yellow with a black capital R attached to the front. This example on the down main line at Finsbury Park was photographed in July 1952. *Author's Collection*

Above right (64a):
These two photographs taken from the end of the down platform at New Barnet illustrate just some of the changes that took place in GNR signalling practice at the end of the 19th century. Here, Stirling 8ft Single No 53 hurries through with an up express in the summer of 1889, seven years before Richard Johnson retired. *E. J. Bedford/National Railway Museum*

Right (64b):
The same location on 20 March 1901 showing the enlarged layout and new up island platform, as Stirling 2-2-2 No 231 approaches with a similar train. The co-acting signals in the 1889 view have survived the reorganisation but have been brought under the control of New Barnet No 2 signalbox (seen on the left), which opened in 1895 to control just the down lines through the station. The spectacle and lamp of the upper of the two arms have been removed, so that it conforms to the arrangement specifically mentioned in Ross's 1902 recommendations for the siting of signals. Notice also the improvement in the permanent way between 1889 and 1901.
The Locomotive Club of Great Britain/ Ken Nunn Collection

A Distant Signal for a signal-box in advance must never overlap a Home or Starting Signal for a signal-box in the rear, but must be fixed on the same post 7ft below the Home or Starting Signal, and be controlled by the Home or Starting Signal, to prevent the Distant arm being off when the Home or Starting arm is at danger. When a Distant Signal is placed below a Home or Starting Signal, no other Signal should be placed on the same post. When the Distant Signals for a Junction have to be combined with the Home or Starting Signals for a signal-box in rear, the Starting Signal post should be nearest the line with the Distant arm for the right hand junction placed under it, and the Distant Signal for the left hand junction should be carried by a separate post to the left of the Home or Starting post. Both Distant arms must be controlled by the Home or Starting Signal. This rule will not apply if the Junction to the right is a Goods or other subordinate line; in this case the Distant Signal should be carried on a separate post to the right of the Home or Starting post.

Lamps

must never be placed nearer together than 7ft with the exception of Bay Starting or other subordinate Signals, for which the lamps may be fixed closer together.

Back Lights

which cannot be seen by the Signalman working the Signals must be dispensed with unless they can be seen from a station platform; in this case they may be retained if it is considered desirable.

Signals

elevated more than 45ft above rail-level signals should have a lower arm worked in connection with the top arm, at an elevation of about 15ft above rail-level, but a single lamp only may be necessary, to be opposite the bottom arm when practicable. *(Pictures 64a and b)*

Signalboxes

should be so placed that the Signalman can see all points and signals from the levers working them, especially facing-points, which must be in all cases clearly seen.

Electric Repeaters

should be avoided as far as possible. If a repeater cannot be avoided, then the Signal should be only sighted at such an elevation as to give the Driver a good sight.

All Signals

should be fixed on the left hand side of, and as near as possible to the road to which they apply. A signal-box or signal placed on a passenger platform must not be at a less distance than six feet from the edge of the platform, and a signal-box or signal must not be erected at a less distance than five feet from any line.

The Representatives

Must each consider the general arrangement of the Signalling. It will be the special duty of the Traffic Representative to see that the signal-box is suitably placed, and that the signals can be seen by the Signalman. It will be the special duty of the Locomotive Representative to see that the Drivers' sight of Signals is good, and that the Signals are fixed at a suitable distance from the fouling points. It will be the duty of the Signal Superintendent to see that the points and signals are placed in such a position as to be satisfactorily worked; are suitably arranged, and are in accordance with the plan.

The changes in GNR signalling practice after 1902 were given added impetus in 1911 by the appointment of Charles J. Brown, who succeeded A. Ross as Chief Engineer, and by the subsequent stringencies forced on the company by World War 1. With so many men away fighting and dying, labour shortages led to immediate economies. The GNR's response to a shortage of staff for routine maintenance work, was to reduce the amount of equipment in use. One of the most obvious changes, which must have been organised very much like a military campaign,

considering its widespread implementation starting on one specific day, was the removal of hundreds of 'directing' distant signals *(Picture 65)*. In line with Board of Trade requirements, these signals had been provided in rear of all junctions off running lines apart from routes into sidings. But starting on 10 May 1915, many of these directing distant signals were removed, the main distant signal being used instead to give advanced warning of a junction by being kept in the on position.

Table 19. The number of directing distant signals removed in 1915	
Main Line Division	113
Eastern Division	23
Western Division	40
West Riding Division	88
GN&GE Joint	6
GN&LNW Joint	2

The changes were swift. On 11 May 1915 for example, the diagram in Werrington Junction signalbox had been altered to show the removal of directing distants previously worked by levers 3, 5, 11, 17, 28, 50, 56, 58 and 70. At many places a mechanical indicator in an adjacent signalbox had displayed to the signalman the aspect of his colleague's distant signal *(Picture 66)*. Until the alterations of 1915, these indicators had displayed the word BLOCKED when the distant signal was in the on position but during 1917 a number had the lettering changed to ON. For some time after the removal of a directing distant signal, the lever still had to be worked as before to operate the indicator. In other places, distant signal arms were left in situ but fixed in the on position. For example, the up main to platform directing distant at Doncaster station was 'fastened at danger' on 22 July 1919. In these cases all connections between signalbox and signal were removed.

An innovation which resulted from the shortages of the war years was the use of reinforced concrete signal posts instead of best red memel or pitch pine masts, which had been specified in the signalling contracts of the 1870s but had become almost unobtainable. The M&GN Joint Railway had first used concrete fence posts in 1909, and William Marriott, the company's Resident Engineer and Locomotive Superintendent, took out a number of patents for signal and telegraph posts, as well as sleepers and other items. As the GNR had been jointly responsible for signalling on this railway, it was not surprising that reinforced concrete signal posts began to appear on the GNR system shortly after they had been successfully erected on the Joint line. Many were supplied by Marriott from the Melton Constable Works of the M&GN Joint Railway and the first reference to the renewal of signal posts on the GNR main line with reinforced concrete examples occurs in 1918, when in July of that year the down main home signal at the flat crossing, Newark, and the down main distant signal at Weston Bank, were replaced. Renewals then continued regularly almost every month up to and beyond the Grouping of 1923 *(Picture 67)*. As well as single

20

West Riding Division continued.

Signal Box.	Present Form.	Description of Directing Distant Signals taken away.	Future Form.
Adwalton Junction		Up Main to Batley Distant	
Wrenthorpe West		Up Main to Leeds Distant. Up Main to Goods Arrival Distant	
Ossett East		Down Main to Down Goods Distant	
Ossett West		Up Main to Up Goods Distant	
Dewsbury Junction		Up Main to Branch Distant	
Dudley Hill Station		Down Main to Loop Distant	
Broad Lane Junction		Down Main to Branch Distant	
Broad Lane Junction		Down Branch to Down Main Distant	
Broad Lane Junction		Up Branch to Up Goods Distant Up Branch to Up Main Distant	
Broad Lane Junction		From Shipley to Branch Distant From Shipley to Up Goods Distant	
Broad Lane Junction		From Laisterdyke to Branch Distant From Laisterdyke to Up Goods Distant	

Left (65):
Just one page of Circular No 30,494a issued by Superintendent of the Line C. J. Selway on 26 April 1915, outlining which directing distant signals were to be removed.
Great Northern Railway Society Collection

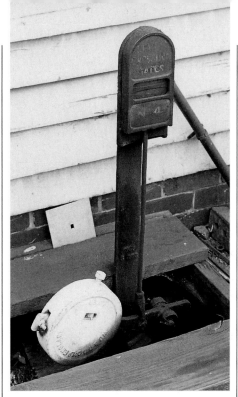

masts, concrete signal brackets were also erected *(Picture 68)* and at a number of level crossings substantial concrete posts were provided on which the gates were hung.

Changes 1920-2

In the 1902 'Instructions as to the Sighting of Signals' document referred to above, there was one particular recommendation which it is very difficult to believe was ever implemented, and that was the positioning of distant signals no more than 900 yards in rear of signalboxes, or 1,100 yards in special circumstances. Attention has already been drawn to the number of distants that by 1877 were over 1,000 yards from the signalboxes operating them, and consequently Ross's ruling must have seemed at the time a retrogressive one, especially on a fast main line such as the GNR. His successor in 1911, Charles Brown, had no objections to siting distants as far out as possible, and after World War 1 he was actively moving distants as well as advanced starting signals to new locations. The latter were resited in response to the running of 80-wagon freight trains[12] and just a few examples will suffice to illustrate Brown's policy:

In the summer of 1920 W. H. Cannon retired as Signal Engineer and was replaced by A. E. Tattersall. While working for the Metropolitan Railway he had installed the first purpose-made two-aspect upper quadrant semaphores in this country (if the possibility that French's original somersault signal was made to give its indication with the arm tilted upwards is discounted) and according to O. S. Nock his intention was to introduce three-position upper quadrant semaphores 'on a considerable scale' on the GNR. If that was his plan, then it never materialised and only six such arms were installed to control the up relief line — formerly the up carriage, — through Gas Works Tunnel, King's Cross. Adjacent to Belle Isle Down Signalbox, one full-size arm was mounted above a route indicator (which could indicate MAIN or LOCAL), and a miniature calling-on arm. Passenger trains could be signalled into the tunnel only by the main arm but empty stock movements were controlled by the miniature arm, which worked to only two positions. At the other end of the tunnel there were two separate posts, each with the same arrangement, the main arms

[12] *Alterations to signalling and to the yard at Ferme Park had been authorised in January 1914.*

giving only two indications and the route indicators in this case displaying platform numbers *(Picture 69)*. A subsidiary colour-light signal was positioned within the tunnel; this, the semaphores and route indicators all being worked from King's Cross West box.

Considering Tattersall's progressive approach to his profession, the decision and timing of the final development in GNR signalling might appear backward looking. At its meeting of 26 January 1922, the Way & Works Committee approved the Engineer's report seeking permission to replace 300 wooden semaphore arms with enamelled iron ones. The report mentioned that existing arms cost about 7s 9d each, with annual painting costing between 2s 0d and 8s 0d per arm. Full-sized plain or fish-tailed (distant) enamelled arms were priced at 16s 9d each, with the shorter examples costing 15s 8d each. For some reason both the full-sized and smaller arms were two inches shorter than their wooden equivalents (58in and 46in respectively) *(Picture 70)*.

The first delivery of the new arms was made in March 1923, just after the Grouping. Special carrying cases were used to transport them to site and Charles Brown, the Engineer, wrote: 'Please see that those responsible have instructions to exercise the greatest care in handling the arms so that they do not chip, and to see that the fan plates are attached with equal care...'

One hundred and seventy-two 58in and 18 46in stop arms were sent for installation on the lines between Potteric Carr and Marshgate, Doncaster, and judging from the photographic

Table 20. Resiting of distant and advance starting signals 1920-2
(NB: This is not a definitive list.)

Signalbox	Signal	Distance from signalbox		Date of
		before	after	Alteration
Bourne West	down distant	759yd	1,356yd	24.10.1920
Essendine South	up main advance and up goods advance	470yd	714yd	12/13.7.1921
Essendine North	up main distant	1,249yd	1,350yd	28.6.1921
Peascliffe	up distant	896yd	2,065yd (worked electrically)	1921

Left (69):
The three-position upper quadrant semaphore immediately south of Gas Works Tunnel, King's Cross, indicating 'line clear' into Platform 5. Despite being a three-position arm, this signal worked to only two positions. This photograph was taken on 5 June 1931 as work on resignalling the terminus was in hand. *LNER/National Railway Museum*

Below left (70):
Detail of the back of a standard full-sized 58in enamelled steel stop arm mounted on a reinforced concrete post at Mablethorpe. The salty seaside atmosphere has obviously taken its toll on the concrete, as the steel reinforcing rods are almost completely exposed at the top of the post. Photograph taken on 4 April 1970. *M. A. King*

Below centre (71):
The reinforced concrete bracket at Firsby East Junction with two examples of the standard 58in enamelled steel stop arms, and a 58in enamelled steel yellow distant arm controlled from Firsby South signalbox. Photograph taken on 13 August 1970. *Geoff Goslin*

Below (72):
The enamelled steel miniature shunting signal at Sleaford West, photographed in the 1960s. *W. H. A. Thompson /D. J. Powell Collection*

Left (73):
Three views of the standard GNR ground disc signal installed at Branston on the GN&GE Joint Railway. Photographed on 30 May 1972, this example had retained its number indicating which lever operated it in the signalbox. The darker disc face was painted red with a red glass to display danger. The lamp case was not attached to the signal and until the use of long-burning lamps, the case and lamp would have been positioned in the disc signal only at night. *M. A. King*

evidence, others were used immediately at King's Cross . The acquisition of enamelled distant signal arms *(Picture 71)* was delayed until the new LNER had made its decision to use yellow as the standard colour for all distant signal arms, while altering the night-time aspect from red to yellow. Charles Brown informed his District Engineers of these changes in a letter dated 26 April 1923 and by the beginning of October that year the replacement of red distant signal spectacle glasses with orange glass, supplied by Messrs Chance of Birmingham, and the repainting of arms had been completed for all signals on the main line between Hougham and Carlton.

Miniature enamelled arms were also manufactured *(Picture 72)*, and eventually a number of GNR ground disc signals were 'modernised' by the addition of two white enamelled discs, one with a central horizontal red stripe and the other, at 90 degrees to it, with an inclined red strip to indicate all clear.

The decision to order enamelled lower quadrant arms at the very end of the GNR's independent existence is a telling example of the division between the responsibilities of Tattersall as Signal Engineer and Brown the Chief Engineer. Tattersall reported to Brown, who made the final decision on mechanical engineering matters, of which signalling had since 1848 always been a part. Tattersall was obviously not in a position to persuade the GNR Board to implement large scale three-position signalling, despite the fact this had been done on the Ealing & Shepherd's Bush Railway just after World War 1, and on the SECR side of Victoria station, London, in 1919/20. The final years of the GNR's independent existence, which saw the introduction of the first of Gresley's influential Pacific locomotives, could be viewed as far as signalling was concerned as a missed opportunity. In December 1929, the LNER informed its staff that from then on, all signal renewals would be with new two position upper quadrant signals.

Ground Disc Signals

The earliest pictorial evidence for the type of ground signal used by the GNR survives in a drawing accompanying documents issued to signalling contractors at the beginning of 1874. Interestingly, the signal was identical to that manufactured by Saxby & Farmer and yet in tender documents of the period it was always referred to as 'GN Pattern Ground Disc'. The lamps and discs of these signals, sometimes referred to as 'point discs', were made to rotate through 90° and were linked directly to the action of the point blades, which meant the two possible aspects depended on the lie of the points. It was soon realised that this was a handicap, as the disc could not tell a driver if the route across the point was unobstructed or not. During the mid-1870s signalling contractors were busy at various locations on the GNR, altering the operation of discs which had only recently been installed by disconnecting them from the point blades and connecting them up to spare levers in the signalbox. For example, in the summer of 1876, Saxby & Farmer charged the GNR £105 7s 1d for 'disconnecting 3 ground discs formerly working with points and connecting them to new wires laid in from the cabin' at Bingham East. When the change from a white to a green all clear aspect was made to all main line signals after the

Abbotts Ripton accident, the glass in ground discs was also changed, this being completed on the North District by August 1878.[13]

Ground discs worked from the signalbox differed from those connected directly to the point blades, by having a counterbalance so that if the wire between it and the lever in the signalbox broke, the disc would automatically return to danger *(Pictures 73a, b and c)*. In this form the GNR ground discs were identical in design to some examples used on the LBSCR. In some locations where the siting of discs needed to be improved, the lamp unit was elevated on its spindle several feet above track level, a feature which was also used by the Highland Railway. An example elevated 6ft above the ground was fixed at Crescent Junction in 1874 and in the contract documentation of May 1882 for signalling on the Leicester to Tilton Junction line, a number of this size were specified. Photographs show that spindles of other lengths were also used in various places *(Picture 74)*.

By 1899, most of the metalwork of ground discs was painted black with the spindle or stem picked out in white. The 'all clear' plate was painted white and the 'danger' plate was painted red; the number of the lever in the signalbox which operated the disc, which was attached to both plates, was usually painted black. This useful form of identification was officially discontinued at the very end of 1921.

Lamps

'All Signal Lamps must be lighted an hour before sunset; and in the event of any dark or foggy weather requiring it they must invariably be lighted, whether the Day Signals can be seen or not.' These were the instructions issued to staff in 1850 and for the next 50 years lamps were regularly extinguished and stored away during the day and then lit again in the evening and taken back to the signals.

The illumination in those early lamps was from candles, the GNR adopting a lamp patented by W. M. Brydone in January 1852. The rights for this lamp were eventually acquired by Stevens & Sons. The candles were supplied by Palmer & Co, the proprietor's reputation being founded on a 'coach candle' lamp he had patented in 1842. For more than a decade Palmer & Co had a monopoly of supplying candles to the GNR but ever cost-conscious, the railway was always looking for other suppliers. In 1867 Palmer's price for a pound weight of candles was 8d and by 1869 at these prices the GNR estimated it was using 60 tons of candles a year at a cost of £4,480. After extensive trials between King's Cross and Potters Bar in January 1869, Price & Co won the contract to supply candles — but the GNR almost immediately regretted the decision when an accident at Retford in the early morning of Sunday 28 February 1869 was caused by a substandard candle (the accident was described in Chapter 2). Although the signalling arrangements were obviously seriously flawed, the GNR put the blame squarely on Price & Co's product and immediately stopped patronising the firm. Palmer & Co once again became the preferred supplier and in July 1871 was providing the railway company with double-wick candles at 7s 0d per dozen and single-wick candles at 6s 6d per dozen.

[13] In the 1912 Appendix to the Book of Rules & Regulations and to the Working Timetables, the danger aspect was noted as a white light.

Above (74):
A pair of ground disc signals with extended spindles at Tumby Woodside, photographed in August 1970. These particular examples had been 'modernised' by the LNER by the addition of enamelled plates. *Geoff Goslin*

In the first years of the 1870s there was an enormous increase in the number of signals in use and by 1874 the GNR estimated it had over 2,000 lamps in service, costing the company £11,200 a year in candles. It was the desire to reduce this expenditure which prompted the next development in signal illumination, rather than any thought for providing a stronger or more reliable light source. In 1873 John Thomas of Barnsbury (half a mile northwest of King's Cross station) took out a patent with Amos Piggott (the GNR's Signal Inspector at Retford) for a lamp that would burn 'petroleum and other mineral oil' (Patent No 2107, 14 June 1873). In that patent Thomas described himself as a lamp manufacturer. Whether or not he was the company's Lamp Foreman at the time is not clear but he certainly was by the time Johnson the Engineer reported on his new invention to the Board in March 1874. Experiments with 21 prototype lamps had been carried out during the winter of 1873/4 at Caledonian Junction and Holloway station, and Johnson had no hesitation in recommending their general adoption, calculating they would save the GNR £6,500 a year.

By the beginning of 1875 there were over 400 of these lamps in use and Thomas was keen to make a financial agreement with his employers for the use of his invention. The GNR, however, dragged its feet on the matter, and in February 1875 he wrote to the company saying: 'I feel bound to say I consider I am not being fairly treated by this delay. The GNR Co are making extensive use of this Patent without seeming to trouble themselves about paying for it...'

Four years later the GNR had 4,500 Thomas Patent lamps in use and only 800 candle lamps, and during that summer (1879) Thomas modified

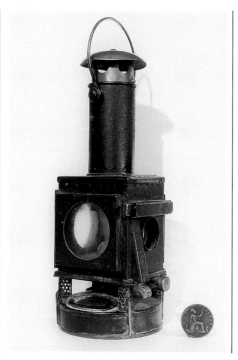

GREAT NORTHERN RAILWAY.

Circular No. 2863a.

PATENT SIGNAL LAMPS FOR BURNING PETROLEUM.

INSTRUCTIONS FOR CLEANING, TRIMMING, AND LIGHTING.

At day-light each morning (except in foggy weather), the Lamps must be taken from the Signal Posts to the Lamp Room.

The inside portion must then be taken from the case, and each part thoroughly cleaned, the burnt portion of the wick being carefully rubbed off and the ash removed with rag or waste.

The Lenses in the outer case must be well cleaned and the vent holes kept open and free from dirt.

The cistern must be filled with Petroleum every morning, and care must be taken that there is always sufficient wick to reach the bottom of the cistern.

To light the Lamp, open it at the lower spring catch; when lighted shut the lamp down again, and regulate the light by means of the milled-edge button.

The Lamp must be lighted at least fifteen minutes before it is put into the outer case, to allow time for the flame to be properly regulated.

The flame must not exceed ⅜ of an inch in height—thus

For Ground Disc Lamps, the flame must not exceed ¼ of an inch in height—thus

At fifteen minutes from the time of lighting the lamp, it may be placed carefully in the outer case and carried to the Signal.

Suitable Petroleum must be provided by the Stores Department, and no other must be used.

The Signalman must report at once to his Station Master and the Signal Inspector, Retford, any defect in the Lamps or Stores supplied.

At intervals of not more than three months the Oil (if any) in the cisterns must be drained off and all sediment and dirt removed therefrom. The Oil thus drained off, after allowing time for any dirt to settle, must not be wasted but be carefully put back in the Lamps, leaving the deposit behind.

A fresh wick must be put in each Lamp at least every three months, care being taken that it be quite dry.

All spare Lamps and wicking are to be kept in a dry place, and all cans, measures and funnels used for Petroleum must not on any account be used for any other oil.

Care must be taken that Petroleum cans and measures are not left where there may be any risk of rain or water getting into them.

Time for Lighting up Semaphore and Disc Signals.

January	...	...	...	3.30 p.m.	July	...	...	7.30 p.m.
February	...	...	...	4.30 „	August	...	...	6.15 „
March	...	...	...	5.15 „	September	...	...	5.15 „
April	...	...	...	6.15 „	October	...	...	4. 0 „
May	...	...	...	7.15 „	November	...	...	3.15 „
June	...	...	...	7.45 „	December	...	...	3. 0 „

FRANCIS P. COCKSHOTT,
Superintendent of the Line.

SUPERINTENDENT'S OFFICE, KING'S CROSS.
March 24th, 1881.

Circular No. 1665a is cancelled.

500 of the former to burn cheaper brands of petroleum, namely Alexandra Brand at 1s 3¼d per gallon. To modify the existing lamps was costed at 3s 0d each but once again Richard Johnson stressed the savings to be made by converting the last of the candle-burning lamps — £6,841pa according to his precise calculations. Thomas was anxious to secure another patent for the modification and Johnson lent him money to achieve this (Patent No 1901, 13 May 1879) *(Picture 75)*. In September 1879 the Way & Works Committee was prepared to be generous and it recommended to the Board that Thomas be paid £200 for costs incurred during the 14 years the patent had been in force.

Gradually the last remaining lamps burning candles were converted, the North District Engineer reporting on 30 April 1881, for example, that petroleum lamps had replaced the candle lamps in the signals at Hougham, Claypole, Newark South, Newark North, Midland Crossing, Carlton and Crow Park. At the very end of that year 400 Thomas patent lamps were purchased from Messrs John Stephenson of Caledonian Road for £1 13s 6d each, indicating that like most GNR signalling equipment, manufacture was in the hands of independent contractors. By this date every lamp case and each interior was numbered and brass plates attached with the name of the signalbox and the signal the lamps were allocated to *(Pictures 76, 77 and 78)*.

It is interesting to note that Thomas's work on the GNR was paralleled by similar but completely independent developments on the LNWR. In 1876, 4,700 oil-burning lamps made to the design of F. W. Webb, the company's Engineer, were brought into use to replace candle lamps. As with Thomas's lamps, they too gradually became the standard form of signal illumination.

Thomas lamps remained in use on the GNR well into the 20th century but the daily chore common to all railway companies of having to position lamps on signals in the evening and then take them in again at daybreak led to the development at the turn of the century of a long-burning lamp which could remain in position and alight for at least a week. The GNR was an early advocate because of the economies it could reap from their use. In September 1908 the Chief Traffic Manager recommended that 2,000 lamps at £1 each should be introduced gradually in the West Riding Division. The savings were calculated to amount to £756 per annum. The experiment was obviously a success and in April 1912 the Traffic Committee agreed to introduce them on the main line between Peterborough and

Right (77):
An example of the lamp case that would have housed a Thomas's patent lamp. Lamp cases of this size were used for main running line signals. Until the first decade of the 20th century both the case and the lamp interior would have only been positioned behind the signal spectacle at night and then brought into the lamp room during the day for trimming and filling. *Harpenden Railway Museum*

Far right (78):
An example of the smaller lamp case used on ground disc signals. This one is plated Marshmoor. *Harpenden Railway Museum*

Shaftholme Junction, recording that approximately 2,000 would be needed but that £800pa would be saved on lamp staff *(Picture 79)*.

Other railway companies were also making the change, the LNWR, for example, deciding in August 1912 that the time was right to introduce 18,096 long burning interiors into their existing lamp cases at a cost of £9,300. By 1923 it had more of these lamps in use than any other railway company. The GWR also became a staunch supporter of long burning lamps and estimated that by 1919 it had over 20,000 in use.

Below (79):
Three sizes of long-burning lamps made to fit standard GNR signal lamp cases. The semicircular notches in the paraffin reservoirs were to avoid the spikes on the lamp brackets which kept the lamp cases in the correct position behind the signals' spectacles (see part No 335 in *Picture 80*). *Harpenden Railway Museum*

Table 21. Signal aspects as outlined in the 1912 Appendix to the Book of Rules & Regulations and the Working Timetables

Distant signal	Danger — red light	With white (spec) back light.
	All Right — green light	With purple (spec) back light.
Home signal	same as above	
Starting signal	Danger — red light	With white (spec) back light to signalbox when the front light cannot be seen from the signalbox.
		No back light when the front light can be seen from the signalbox.
	All Right — green light	With purple (spec) back light to signalbox when the front light cannot be seen from the signalbox.
		No back light when the front light can be seen from the signalbox.
Advanced starting signal	Danger — red light	No back light.
	All Right — green light	No back light.
Disc signal	Danger	Will show white (spec) front light, and white (spec) back light to signalbox when the front light cannot be seen from the signalbox.
		No back light when the front light can be seen from the signalbox.
	All Right — green light	No back light.

The lights of ground disc signals which work in connection with semaphore signals to be similar to the lights of semaphore signals.

NB: Where the lights are electrically repeated to the signalbox and where the front lights are visible from the signalbox, the back lights in the signal lamps to be blocked out and no back spectacles provided, except at places where back light and back spectacles are found useful for the guidance of Level Crossing Gatekeepers or others.

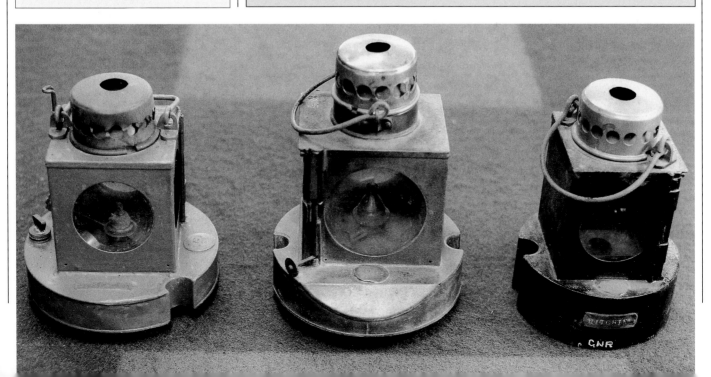

5. The Signalling Contractors

Unlike the LNWR, the MR or the GWR, who manufactured most of their own mechanical and electrical signalling equipment, the GNR always relied very heavily on signalling contractors to supply and fit the majority of its signalling hardware *(Picture 80)*.

Stevens & Sons, Darlington Works, Southwark Bridge Road, London

The first contractor the company turned to was Stevens & Sons, simply because it was the only one specialising in railway signalling equipment in the 1840s and 50s. The GNR was obviously not comfortable with this monopoly and a complaint about high prices in December 1854 led the Executive & Traffic Committee to ask the General Manager to obtain prices from other 'signal makers'. By the mid-1860s the GNR was able to obtain tenders for 'signal fittings' from a number of new firms, including J. Pears, Yardley & Co, P. & W. McLelland, Jukes Coulston & Co and Gunson & Co, but even then Stevens still managed to offer the lowest prices. Stevens was also able to provide the GNR with the railway company's first interlocking apparatus. It was not until the end of the decade that the firm faced serious competition from new organisations entering a steadily expanding railway signalling

market, and when this happened the GNR had no compunction in giving work to others. In November 1867, for example, Saxby & Farmer undercut Stevens by a mere 7s to win the contract to supply and fit the new locking apparatus at the north end of Hatfield station — £449 13s as opposed to £450!

Ironically, after so many years as the only supplier, as soon as the demand for locking apparatus increased in the 1870s, Stevens & Sons found it secured far fewer GNR contracts. King's Cross station was signalled by the firm in 1872/3 but the decade was otherwise a lean one for Stevens *(Picture 81)*, despite its equipment being

Table 22. Tenders for signalling work, 1867-8

Wortley Junction locking apparatus — December 1867

E. S. Yardley & Co, Manchester	£535 4s	
Saxby & Farmer, London	£267	
Stevens & Sons, Southwark	£236	(successful tender)

Welwyn Junction locking apparatus — December 1867

E. S. Yardley & Co	£434 7s	
Saxby & Farmer	£211 10s	
Stevens & Sons	£195	(successful tender)

Hitchin Junction (Cambridge Junction) locking apparatus — January 1868

E.S. Yardley & Co	£407	
Vickers, Sons & Co, Sheffield	£370	
Saxby & Farmer	£283 10s	
Stevens & Sons	£250	(successful tender)

Grantham Junction locking apparatus — November 1868

Vickers, Sons & Co	£250	
McKenzie, Clunes & Holland Worcester	£212 12s 6d	
Yardley, Sons & Co	£181 1s 6d	
Stevens & Sons	£180	
Saxby & Farmer	£175	(successful tender)

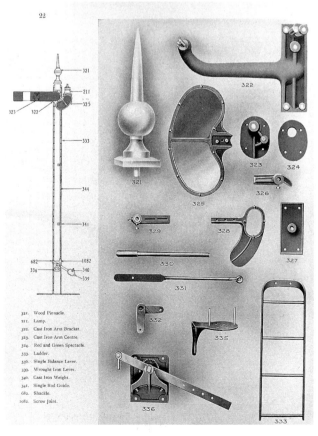

22

321. Wood Pinnacle.
211. Lamp.
322. Cast Iron Arm Bracket.
323. Cast Iron Arm Centre.
324. Red and Green Spectacle.
333. Ladder.
336. Single Balance Lever.
330. Wrought Iron Lever.
340. Cast Iron Weight.
341. Single Rod Guide.
682. Shackle.
1082. Screw Joint.

of a technical and materials standard equivalent to the other important signalling contractors[14]. In 1881 it tendered for three large jobs — the resignalling of Spalding station, work at Hammerton Street Junction, and the resignalling of the Spalding & March line. The income for the firm had it been successful would have been almost £12,000 but the work went elsewhere. There was some small compensation early the following year when it was given the work of replacing a number of lever frames in the Yorkshire District at £210 each.

Easterbrook & Co, London

Of the new generation of contractors vying for Stevens's work, Easterbrook & Co was one of the first the GNR employed early in the 1870s. In 1871 the firm secured the contracts to fit two locking frames, each with 30 levers, at Doncaster and another at Three Signal Bridge, Leeds, which was brought into use on 27 May 1872. At the end of that year attention turned to Wortley West Junction and in April 1873 Johnson reported that the contract for providing the locking apparatus on the Ossett Branch could be 'safely' given to Easterbrook & Co. In 1874 the firm was busy fitting frames into 10 signalboxes at Tuxford, Essendine North and South (Picture 82), Great Ponton, Tallington, Bingham East & West, Armley, Bramley and Stanningley. The following year it fixed a frame in Radcliffe-on-Trent signalbox and another with 26 levers in Honington Junction.

But satisfaction with Easterbrook's equipment was short-lived and in 1876 the frame in Tallington was giving problems. After that no more contracts were awarded to the firm and at the Way & Works Committee meeting of 31 July 1883 Johnson reported that 'At Essendine we are

[14] It is ironic that tappet locking developed by Stevens & Sons in 1870 eventually became the preferred type in all other signalling contractors' frames, many having their original form of locking removed and replaced by tappet locking.

fixing Saxby & Farmer Locking frames at both ends of the station, in place of those which we fixed in early days, and were not considered quite safe in working.'

In November that year Walter Easterbrook started an action against the GNR '...to recover damages for the infringement of their patent for making locking apparatus'. This was one of a number of similar actions against railway companies but aimed at Saxby & Farmer, who Easterbrook believed had infringed his patent of 1867 (No 927) for catch-handle locking. The case with the GWR was used as the test and with some relief the GNR's Way & Works Committee recorded in July 1885 that Easterbrook's action against the GWR had failed.

Ransomes & Rapier, Ipswich

Long before Easterbrook & Co had been quietly abandoned by the company, Ransomes & Rapier had seemed to the GNR to be the most cost-effective contractor in the market. In October 1872, Johnson the company's Engineer enthusiastically drew the Way & Works Committee's attention to a new type of locking apparatus invented by that firm, and suggested that two sets should be bought for trial purposes, because in his opinion '...they are the best and simplest apparatus of the kind which have yet been produced and the price, £7 per lever, is rather less than that of the other makers'. During the next two years at least 30 frames were installed on the main line and on the Lincolnshire Loop line. Most had no more than 35 levers but in 1873 an 80-lever frame was installed in Pelham Street Crossing signalbox at Lincoln (Picture 83). Johnson admitted later that he had tried to reduce the total to 60, as the number of levers in a box sometimes frightened him. Once convinced, however, he felt confident in recommending to the Way & Works Committee in April 1874 that no more work should be given to Saxby & Farmer or Easterbrook & Co, and that Ransomes & Rapier's frames should be used from then on, especially as they were guaranteed

for 10 years. In the end, although the frames proved very robust and long-lived, as described in Chapter 2, their simplicity that had endeared them to Johnson was not up to new demands for conditional and sequential locking in later years and no more were fitted into signalboxes after 1880.

Saxby & Farmer, Patent Railway Signal Works, Canterbury Road, Kilburn, London

Without a doubt, the firms that secured the most work from the GNR during the 1870s and were able to offer the latest technology at very competitive prices, were Saxby & Farmer and McKenzie, Clunes & Holland. The earliest known Saxby & Farmer GNR contract has already been mentioned but how much more work the firm secured between then and the well-documented period from 1874 onwards is not known. Peterborough received Saxby & Farmer frames in 1872 but these were obviously very soon replaced because two years later the firm returned to install new frames in Crescent Junction, Peterborough North, Spital Junction, Westwood Junction, New England North, Walton Crossing and Werrington Junction, all this work being completed by 1876.

During the same period the firm was employed at Grantham (South, Yard and North Boxes), Retford (South and North), Doncaster (Black Carr Junction, 'A', 'B' and 'C' Boxes), and frames were installed into seven new signalboxes on the Grantham and Nottingham Branch. In the January 1876 contract details for work at Barnet and Hadley Wood, Saxby & Farmer included an engraving of its 1874 Patent (No 294) 'Rocker' frame complete with an inscription declaring 'The Apparatus, on this principle, at Waterloo Bridge Terminus of the L&SWR consists of 109 levers the largest ever made.' (Picture 84)

Far left (80):
All the major signalling contractors could supply the GNR with somersault signals and this was the relevant page in the Railway Signal Co's trade catalogue of 1909.
Transport Trust Library

Left (81):
This Stevens & Sons 40-lever frame was brought into use in Mablethorpe signalbox on 16 October 1877. The two levers which have been reversed (ie pulled forward in the frame) show the different 'travel' of the point and signal levers very well. Point levers had the shortest travel. The first McKenzie & Holland and Saxby & Farmer frames, including the latter's 'Rocker & Gridiron' type, also had this anomaly. Visible in the foreground of this January 1970 photograph is the Tyer's No 7 single line tablet instrument (see Chapter 7).
J. G. Glover

Right (82):
Contemporary lithograph of one of the lever frames supplied by Easterbrook & Co for the signalboxes at Essendine. This illustration shows the locking which would have been hidden beneath the operating room floor at the front of the signalbox in the locking room. The contract to supply the frames was won in October 1872 but the signalboxes did not open until June 1874. Peter Kay Collection

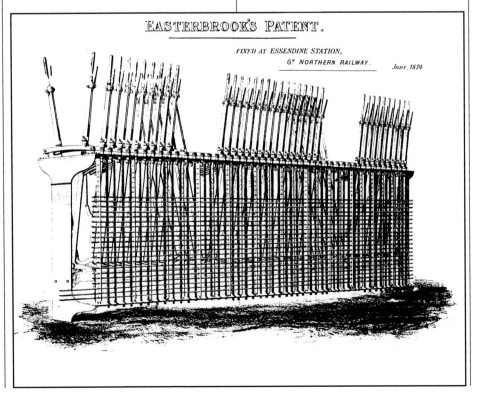

EASTERBROOK'S PATENT.

FIXED AT ESSENDINE STATION, GT NORTHERN RAILWAY.
June, 1874.

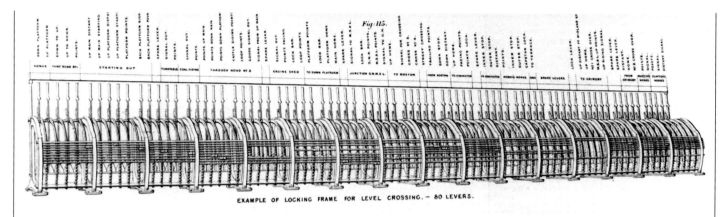

EXAMPLE OF LOCKING FRAME FOR LEVEL CROSSING. – 80 LEVERS.

McKenzie, Clunes & Holland (McKenzie & Holland after 1873), Vulcan Ironworks, Shrub Hill, Worcester

McKenzie & Holland also prospered in the early 1870s and in March 1874 the Executive Committee proposed that the firm should be employed '...for general signal works on the Line, special tenders being obtained for larger works'. As with most things, the GNR's inability to stay with a decision for more than a year meant that within months McKenzie & Holland had won the very large contract in January 1875 to signal the first section of the GNR's new Derbyshire Extension Lines between Colwick and Pinxton for £16,400. By the time Capt Tyler came to inspect the work for the Board of Trade in July 1876, the firm had installed a total of 337 levers into 16 new signalboxes. On the strength of this work the resignalling of Barkston South went to McKenzie & Holland but, interestingly, despite Johnson's satisfaction with the Colwick-Pinxton work, his recommendation to use the firm to signal the rest of the Derbyshire Extension Lines when completed to Egginton Junction just north of Burton upon Trent the following year was ignored and Saxby & Farmer won the contract for that job.

Gloucester Wagon Co

The London and Worcester firms, however successful, never quite managed to divide the GNR's contracts between themselves. In December 1876, the Gloucester Wagon Co submitted its first tender for the signalling of Ayot St Peters — £818. McKenzie & Holland undercut that bid by £133 to win the contract for £685 but after just one other unsuccessful tender (for the resignalling of Hitchin station in March 1877), the Gloucester Wagon Co was awarded the contract in September that year for work at Kirton station in Lincolnshire for £750, (McKenzie & Holland's price had been £910). A

far bigger project was landed in May 1878, when the firm won the contract to build two signalboxes and equip three on the Newark and Bottesford branch for £1,895 *(Picture 85)*. The job was completed extremely rapidly and brought into use at the end of June that same year. After that, work was thin on the ground and the firm was last employed by the GNR in 1882 at Finsbury Park and Hornsey.

Williams Railway Patents Co and Tweedy & Co, Carlisle

The 1880s, as with the previous decade, were dominated by Saxby & Farmer and McKenzie & Holland. Other firms occasionally won contracts but they must have wondered if it was worth their while tendering. During this period a few unfamiliar names occur; for example, in March 1881 Williams Railway Patents Co tendered for signalling work at Firsby. Its bid of £894 3s 6d was the highest by a long way, almost exactly twice as much as Saxby & Farmer's successful price of £447 12s 10d. The firm tried again at the end of the year with a bid for work at 20th Mile and Digswell but once again came in with the highest tender. A little later Tweedy & Co put in a huge bid of £9,670 1s 8d for signalling the Leen Valley line in Nottinghamshire but the work went to Saxby & Farmer for £6,070 16s 7d. Despite their efforts, neither Williams Railway Patents Co nor Tweedy & Co managed to win any GNR contracts.

Dutton & Co, Shrub Hill, Worcester

What helped boost the signalling market at the end of the 1880s was the 1889 Regulation of Railways Act, forcing every railway company to complete the interlocking of all its passenger lines. One of the first new firms able to reap the benefits of this requirement was Dutton & Co. After a long career with McKenzie & Holland, Samuel Telford Dutton set up his own manufacturing business in 1888, immediately adjacent to his former employers in Worcester. He made his first bid for a GNR contract in the spring of 1890, tendering unsuccessfully (£8,049) for the resignalling of St Albans, Ayot, Wheathampstead, New Mill End, Luton, Dunstable, Cole Green and Hertford stations. The firm's first successful tender was an impressive £14,652 16s 9d, accepted by the GNR in July 1893 for the signalling of Holloway Carriage Sidings. Dutton & Co was employed again during the next few years *(Picture 86)*, but the contracts never really compared with the Holloway work.

Evans O'Donnell & Co, Chippenham

Another new firm to emerge in this period was Evans O'Donnell & Co, which entered the fray in 1894, manufacturing from a site at Chippenham on the GWR main line. Its first attempt to secure work from the GNR was made in March 1895, when it tendered for signalling work at New Barnet involving the erection of New Barnet No 2 Signalbox. The bid of £6,454 2s 9d was the highest of five and the firm was not employed. Three months later it tendered, unsuccessfully, for work at Doncaster, and then over the next two years it regularly submitted prices *(Picture 87)*. The manipulation of prices did occasionally impinge upon the GNR tendering process and in November 1897 it effected one of Evans O'Donnell's bids. In that month the Way & Works Committee accepted Saxby & Farmer's tender for signalling the first section of the Leen Valley Extension, as long as the firm agreed to a discount of 2.5%, which it did. This in effect reduced the price to below that of the actual lowest tender, which had come from Evans O'Donnell. Significantly, the company was successful only two months later in January 1898, when it won the contract to resignal between Offord and Ouse Signalboxes, between Abbotts Ripton and 62nd Mile, and from Arlesey to Hitchin, for £2,033 15s 6d. One further contract followed in 1899 and the firm's final work for the GNR was the signalling of the northern section of the Leen Valley Extension between Pleasley Colliery and Langwith Junction, opened in 1901.

The Railway Signal Co, Fazakerley

The firm that eventually had an impact on the GNR approaching that of Saxby & Farmer and McKenzie & Holland in the 1870s and '80s, was The Railway Signal Co. It had been founded in 1881 when George Edwards had left the Gloucester Wagon Co to work for himself and within a matter of months his new firm had tendered successfully (£420) for signalling work at 20th Mile and Digswell, accepted by the GNR at the beginning of December 1881. After that rapid start, however, the GNR gave the company very little work over the next 20 years. It occasionally undercut Saxby & Farmer and McKenzie & Holland's prices by significant margins, as it did in May 1888, for example, when the difference between the two older firms' prices for signalling the new junction at Nottingham (Trent Lane) was only £40 4s, whereas the difference in the Railway Signal Co's successful tender was £384 less than

Table 23. Extracts from Dutton & Co's signalling contract for Holloway Carriage Sidings, June 1893

GNR labour to build Holloway Carriage Sidings box.
148 new signal arms on one existing and three new gantries and two
    existing and 20 new brackets.

368 new working and 57 new spare levers.	£3 2s each.
33 slotting apparatus.	
31 ground disc signals.	£2 7s 6d each.
157, 2ft and 194 1.5ft wire stretching screws.	
22 facing point locks with fittings.	£12
162 wrought-iron vertical cranks, 14in square.	17s each
179 flat adjusting cranks, 10in x 9in.	15s 6d each
233 ditto non-adjusting.	13s
168 side cranks for wires.	12s 6d each

Day Work:

24 foremen per day	12s 6d each
100 fitters per day	8s each
100 labourers per day	5s each
50 smiths per day	9s each
50 strikers per day	5s each
carpenters per day	8s each
labourers per day	5s each
painters per day	7s
painters labourer per day	4s 6d
bricklayers per day	8s
bricklayers labourer per day	5s
general labourers per day	4s 6d

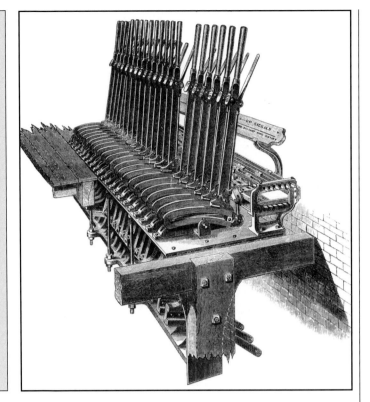

Saxby & Farmer's bid of £2,251 16s. It was not until the late 1890s and the turn of the century that it really made its presence felt on the GNR by winning almost all signalling contracts on offer, squeezing out both old and new hands (*Picture 88*).

Table 24. Standard GNR mechanical equipment specified in 1880s and '90s contracts

The following items were specified in the documentation sent to signalling contractors tendering for the Tilton and Leicester line contract in May 1882.

GN Boston pattern wire adjusters
GN pattern repeating indicators in signalbox
GN pattern ground discs
GN pattern 1¼in point adjusting screws
GN pattern wrought-iron compensating levers
GN pattern gongs

J. F. Pease & Co Ltd, Middlesbrough

J. F. Pease & Co Ltd was one of the last of the new names in signalling contracting, having taken over Dutton & Co at the end of 1899. The supply and fitting of traditional mechanical equipment, however, was a short-lived enterprise, the firm selling out to McKenzie & Holland in October 1901. But in that short space of time it tendered (unsuccessfully) for five GNR signalling jobs — December 1899, signalling the new down slow line between Finsbury Park and Wood Green, £9,549 3s 4d; April 1900, signalling the Leen Valley Extension, £3,132 4s 6d; May 1900, signalling the down lines at Holloway, £4,194 13s 1d; June 1900, signalling work at Biggleswade, £3,878 3s 10d; and October 1900, new 40-lever frame for Shipley Signalbox, £166.

The W. R. Sykes Interlocking Co, Voltaire Road, Clapham, London

The Sykes Interlocking Co first began to supply and fit mechanical equipment in 1903 but the firm's roots stretched back a long way and the business was based on the reputation established by William Sykes, who had devised the first reliable lock & block system in the 1880s, based

Above (84):
The engraving of a Rocker & Gridiron lever frame which Saxby & Farmer included in its contract details supplied to the GNR in 1876.
Author's Collection

Below (85):
Cotham signalbox on the Newark & Bottesford branch, built and equipped by the Gloucester Wagon Co, was brought into use in June 1878. This photograph was probably taken in the first decade of the 20th century.
Nottingham Local Studies Library

Above (86):
Finsbury Park No 2 signalbox opened early in 1875, this Dutton & Co 75-lever frame replacing the original locking apparatus in 1894. The frame was photographed in July 1973, nine months before it was removed.
J. Howard Turner/Signalling Record Society

Above right (87):
The north end of the Evans O'Donnell 35-lever frame in Gainsborough (Lea Road) signalbox, photographed in November 1981. The signalling contractor's name can just be made out cast into the end quadrant plate nearest the camera. The frame was installed in 1895 to replace the original Saxby & Farmer locking apparatus of 1877. *John Dixon*

Below (88):
A 1948 photograph of part of the Railway Signal Co 105-lever frame which had been installed in Grantham North signalbox in 1903. Although all the original GNR description plates (lever leads) had been replaced with 'traffolite' examples, LNER emergency releases for lever locks are prominent on the block shelf and the track diagram is an LNER illuminated one, the box interior still retained a very strong GNR atmosphere. *Clifford F. Buttery*

Right (143):
Balne Lane, photographed in the 1960s. The box closed on 29 November 1970.
Robert Humm Collection

West Riding Signalboxes

It has already been shown that West Riding signalboxes differed considerably from their southern contemporaries, and drawings issued from Leeds Engineer's Department from the late 1880s show that the District continued to produce its own distinctive designs. The official drawing dated 15 July 1886 for the all-timber signalbox at Batley West showed prominent boarding above the operating room windows in place of top lights. The locking room had horizontal lapped boarding, while that in the gable end was vertical. (This signalbox was also unique in being perched on one side of a wrought-iron frame straddling both tracks next to a road overbridge.) Another drawing dated 11 October 1887 for the proposed timber signalbox at Holbeck shows a Type 1b/Top Light design but with the space where the top lights would have been filled with vertical lapped boarding. In this example the boarding of the gable ends was horizontal to match the locking room. The same arrangement was used much later for the signalbox at Howden Clough opened in 1896. It cannot be said with any certainty just how many signalboxes were built to this design, but echoes of the Type 1b/Top Light design were found in signalboxes at Lofthouse North (1891) and Laisterdyke East Junction (1892), Pudsey Lowtown (1893) and Wrenthorpe West (1901), built by the Kell Brothers for £195.

Type 1b/Balne Lane: 1890-c1904

Characteristics:
Operating room window sash units (movable and fixed) either three panes high by two panes wide (3) or two panes high by two panes wide (2); narrow window/top light over the operating room door; earth closet cantilevered out at the rear of the box at operating room level; in the examples with brick locking rooms, the timber boarding in the gable ends extended the full width of the structure. (As in previous tables, dated official plan and elevations survive for signalboxes marked with an asterisk.)

Name	Date Opened	Notes
West Riding & Grimsby Joint Railway		
Balne Lane [1]	1892	(3)
Beeston Junction	3.6.1890	(3); all-timber structure, all boarding horizontal; decorative barge board four semicircles connected by plain timber.
Wortley South	1895	(3); operating room glazed on all elevations; decorative barge board a variation of that shown on the 1874 drawing.
Leeds 'A' *[2]	1904	(3); drawing undated.
Hunslet Branch		
Parkside*	3.7.1899	(3); drawing dated 26 January 1899; all-timber structure.
Hunslet*	3.7.1899	(3); drawing undated; all-timber structure.
Holbeck to Laisterdyke & Bradford via Stanningley		
Wortley West*	c9.1893	(3); drawing dated 26 April 1893; the elevation shows window sash units only one pane wide by three panes high, but this is certainly the draughtsman's shorthand.
Armley Moor	c9.1893	(2)
Bramley West*	c9.1893	(2); drawing dated 25 April 1893.
Shipley Branch		
Shipley Junction	19.5.1901	(3)
Bramley to Low Moor		
Pudsey Greenside*	1893	(2); drawing dated 17 April 1893.

[1] — *Picture 143*
[2] — *Picture 144*

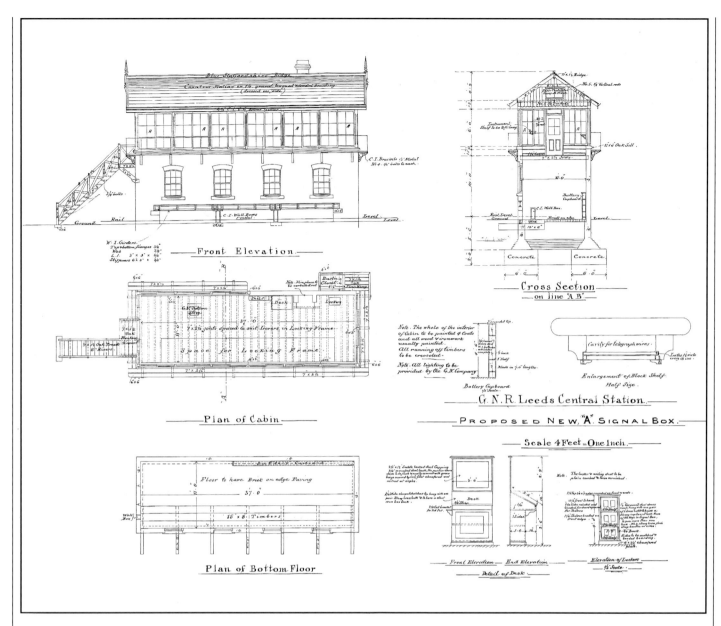

Type 1/revivals: 1883-98

The Type 1b/Balne Lane was the last distinctive Type 1 design of which a significant number were built. During the same period the GNR revived (or continued to use, according to some authorities) a number of its earlier designs, usually because it wanted the new buildings to resemble existing adjacent signalboxes. There were notable exceptions, of course. Lowfield signalbox opened in January 1887 just south of Newark on the Bottesford branch, for example, was built to the Type 1b/Stow Park design (without locking room windows in recessed panelling on the front elevation), yet the other boxes on the branch were of the Type 1b/1875 drawing (Yorks & Notts) and its derivative the Type 1b/Barkston South. No attempt was made to change the decorative barge board to match either. It is interesting to note that barely 20 miles away in the same county, in the same year, the GNR provided a Type 2 signalbox (opened 1 October 1887) for the station at Bulwell Forest.

Type 1a/Arlesey (revival)

Name	Date Opened	Notes
Main Line		
St Neots South[1]	20.4.1898	An all-timber structure built to replace the 1877 South box and match St Neots North also of 1877 which was retained (but reframed) during the resignalling of 1898; the new box had window sash units of four panes high by three panes wide.

[1]*Picture 146*

Type 1b/Doncaster (revival)

Signalboxes in this category were classified by the Signalling Study Group as Type 1/Decoy. Main windows were made up of sashes (movable or fixed) two panes wide by four high, grouped in pairs. Unless otherwise stated, boxes had locking room windows set into recessed brick panelling.

Name	Date Opened	Notes
Main Line		
Babworth	16.5.1892	
Canal	16.5.1892	All-timber.

Name	Date Opened	Notes
Main Line		
Decoy No 1	1.9.1895	Roof pitch not as steep as other Type 1b/Doncaster; vertical boarding operating room floor to roof on rear elevation.
Decoy No 2	11.8.1895	Roof pitch not as steep as other Type 1b/Doncaster; glazed on all elevations.
Carr	12.7.1891	Roof pitch not as steep as other Type 1b/Doncaster.
Balby Junction	10.5.1883	
Shakespeare	8.6.1891	Roof pitch not as steep as other Type 1b/Doncaster
Shaftholme Junction	25.1.1892	

Type 1b/1875 drawing (Yorks & Notts) (revival)

Those structures built in the West Riding after 1883 differed from their pre-1883 family members by having a prominent window/top light over the door to the operating room, and by having window sash units three not four panes high. As elsewhere when listing West Riding signalboxes, those marked * have been identified from official elevations and plans.

Name	Date Opened	Notes
Waltham, Eaton & Eastwell Branches		
Wycombe Junction	18.4.1887	Two locking room windows.
West Riding & Grimsby Joint Railway		
Hampole*	1897	Drawing not dated but has pencil note 'constructed 1897 by Messrs Arnold & Son'; window sash units three panes high by two panes wide.
Lofthouse South*[1]	1897	Drawing not dated, and was a mirror image of the finished signalbox; window sash units three panes high by two panes wide.
West Riding Branches		
Flushdyke*	1891	Drawing not dated, and was a mirror image of the finished signalbox; window sash units three panes high by two panes wide.
Laisterdyke to Halifax via Bowling		
Hall Lane	1886	No window/top light over the door to the operating room, horizontal boarding in the gable ends, and window sash units standard four panes high by two panes wide.

[1] — *Picture 146*

Above left (144):
Official elevations and plan of Leeds 'A' signalbox, produced by the Engineer's Department in Leeds.
John Cockcroft Collection

Below left (145):
St Neots (South), photographed on 16 September 1974. This signalbox took over control of the complete station layout at the end of November 1925 when the North box closed. It was abolished itself on 10 December 1977. *M. A. King*

Below right (146):
Lofthouse South Junction signalbox, photographed in the 1960s before it closed on 21 November 1965. At the current state of research, no other signalbox is known to have been fitted with this particular design of decorative barge board.
Robert Humm Collection

Type 1b/Stow Park (revival)

Name	Date Opened	Notes
Main Line		
Finsbury Park (No 5)	3.1888	
East Lincolnshire Railway		
Willoughby station	23.9.1886	Standard window sash units three panes high by two panes wide in three groups of three on the front elevation, but with sash units three panes high by three panes wide on the non-staircase gable end; three brick panels long.
St Dunstans to Keighley		
Denholme	1.1.1884	Locking room and back wall constructed of stone 'bricks'.
Ingrow [1]	1.1.1884	

[1] Picture 147

Left (147):
Ingrow signalbox, photographed in 1952, three years before it was officially closed in June 1955. *D. Ibbotson*

Below left (148):
Billingborough North signalbox, photographed in the early years of the 20th century. The box closed on 28 February 1959.
R. Tarpey Collection

Signalbox Colours

As a postscript to this section of the chapter, it is possible to give the standard colours that signalboxes were painted in this period because a circular of March 1899 from A. Ross, the Engineer, survives, listing the colours to be used on all GNR buildings. The paint descriptions are those given in the official circular. When the signalbox was an all-timber structure, the lower section (which was officially 4ft above rail level but obviously varied according to the Districts), was painted chocolate, with a 1½in black band separating it from the rest of the woodwork which was finished in light and dark stone. Window sashes were painted light green. Doors and door frames were chocolate with light brown panels. Steps were light and dark stone, with chocolate downpipes, but all other metalwork was black. Where wooden nameboards with cast-iron letters were used instead of the earlier blue enamel plates with white letters, the background was black with a white inner border and a red outer one and the letters picked out in white. Inside the operating room, the lower part of the walls to dado or window sill level was painted chocolate but no colour was specified for the rest of the walls. Any internal woodwork was painted light and dark stone.

Signalboxes 1907-23

Once the widening of the lines in Yorkshire and within 10 miles of London had been completed by the early years of the 20th century, the number of new signalboxes constructed dropped noticeably. As mentioned elsewhere, 1902 was the year when the GNR appointed its first Signal Superintendent, charged with the task of

Type 1b/Gainsborough (revival)

Name	Date Opened	Notes
Bourne & Sleaford Branch		
Billingborough North[1]	7.9.1891	Plain barge boards.

Although this author has been unable to find photographs of the other six signalboxes on the Bourne and Sleaford Branch, it is reasonable to assume that as all were opened at the same time as Billingborough North, they were all built to exactly the same design.

[1] *Picture 148*

establishing network-wide standards of signalling. There are no documentary references to the introduction of a standard signalbox, but an official set of plans and elevations survive for the new signalbox at Moorhouse in the West Riding Division *(Picture 149)*, the box opening in 1907. The drawing shows a design of signalbox which with the benefit of hindsight we know became the new standard. It is significant that the drawing was issued from the Engineer's Department in Leeds, which for so long had pro-

duced its own very distinctive signalbox types. Obviously by 1907, A. Ross the GNR's Chief Engineer had managed to bring all the Divisions into line.

In 1909 all-timber versions of this new design were provided on the extension of the Enfield branch. The design (both timber and brick) was derived from the Type 3 but incorporated narrower panes of glass in the window sash units and had noticeably deep barge boards. The Signalling Study Group designated it the Type 4,

and divided the category into two subgroups, according to whether the barge boards were 'decorative' (Type 4a) or plain (Type 4b). The decorative pattern was another variation of the 'three hole' type similar to pattern four used on Type 1b/Saxondale, although cruder. As with the Type 3 boxes, the window sash units were all four panes high but were made up of units, two, four and five panes wide. For convenience, this author has listed the brick and timber signalboxes separately with appropriate subdivision.

Type 4a/brick

Characteristics:
'Three hole' pattern barge board; earth closet cantilevered out from the back of the box '+'; details from official drawing '*'.

Name	Date Opened	Notes
Main Line		
Essendine North	1913	Glazed on all elevations; two two-pane-wide sash units at either end and in the centre of the track-side elevations; other sash units four panes wide; box five window units long.
Bytham[1]	1912	Front elevation made up of 12 two-pane-wide sash units.
Corby Glen	1912	Front elevation made up of 12 two-pane-wide sash units.
Bawtry	1911	Two two-pane-wide sash units at either end of the front elevation with three four-pane-wide sash units in between; five window sections long.
East Lincolnshire Railway		
Bellwater Junc	1.1913	+; front elevation glazing made up of six three-pane-wide sash units.
'New Line' — Coningsby to Bellwater Junction		
(Signalboxes built by the contractors of the line Messrs Harold Arnold & Sons for £1,185.)		
Coningsby	1.7.1913	+
Tumby Woodside	1.7.1913	+; front elevation glazing made up of six two-pane-wide sash units.
New Bolingbroke	1.7.1913	+; front elevation glazing made up of eight two-pane-wide sash units.
Stickney	1.7.1913	+; front elevation glazing made up of eight two-pane-wide sash units.
Midville	1.7.1913	Front elevation glazing made up of eight two-pane-wide sash units.
Spilsby Road	1.7.1913	Ground level crossing box; front elevation glazing made up of six two-pane-wide sash units.
Eastern Loop Line — Peterborough to Doncaster		
Coningsby Junc	1912	Front elevation glazing made up of eight two-pane-wide sash units.
West Riding & Grimsby Joint Railway		
Moorhouse*	1907	Front elevation glazing made up of eight two-pane-wide sash units.

[1] *Picture 150*

Type 4a/timber

Characteristics:
Horizontal lapped boarding; 'three hole' pattern barge board; front elevation glazing made up of six two-pane-wide sash units unless stated otherwise.

Name	Date Opened	Notes
Main Line		
Loversall Carr[1]	17.5.1909	Two two-pane-wide sash units at either end of the front elevation with three four-pane-wide sash units in between; five window sections long.
Enfield Branch		
Grange Park	26.4.1909	+
Enfield	1910	
Gordon Hill	4.4.1910	
Crews Hill	4.4.1910	
Cuffley	4.4.1910	

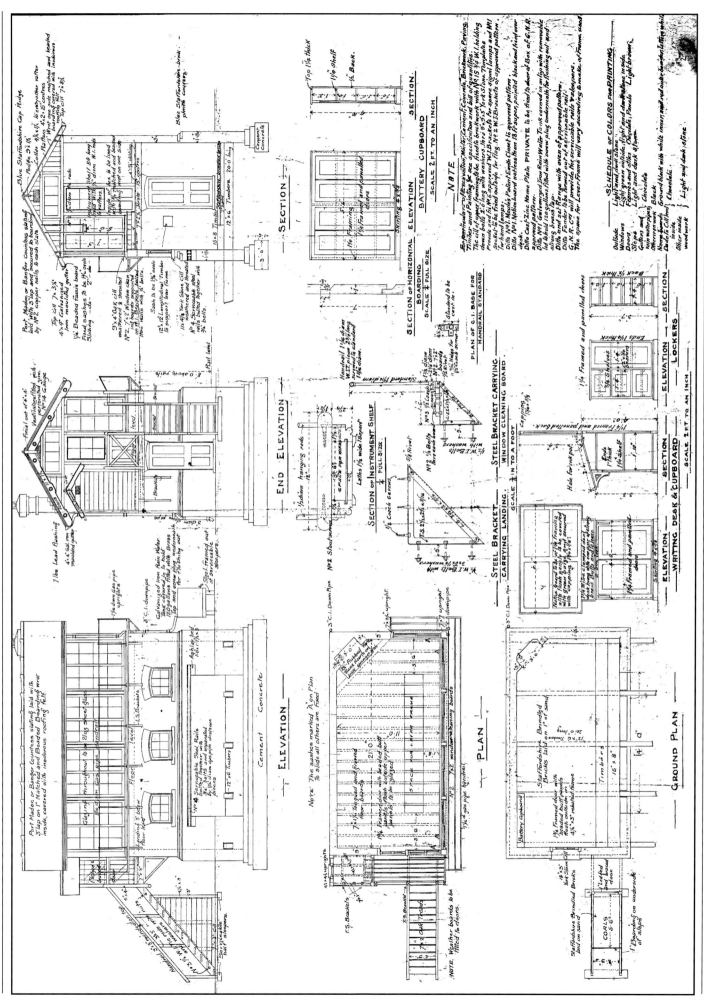

104

Name	Date Opened	Notes
Hitchin and Cambridge Branch		
Letchworth	1913	+; box erected by local builder, M. J. Allen & Sons for £266 18s.

[1]Picture 151

Type 4b/brick

Characteristics:
Plain barge board.

Name	Date Opened	Notes
Main Line		
Langley	11.1912	Glazed on all elevations; two two-pane-wide sash units at either end of both the main and branch line elevations, with an additional two-pane-wide movable sash unit on both elevations; six window sections long (three being four-pane-wide sash units).
Barnby Don Branch		
Skellow*	1916	Drawing dated 18 October 1915; two two-pane-wide sash units at either end of the front elevation with four four-pane-wide sash units in between; six window sections long.
Eastern Loop Line — Peterborough to Doncaster		
Spalding No 1	1921	
Spalding No 2	c3.1921	Two two-pane-wide sash units at either end of the front elevation with four five-pane-wide sash units in between; six window sections long.
Five Mile House	3.1920	Two two-pane-wide sash units at either end of the front elevation with one five-pane-wide sash unit in between; three window sections long.

The Type 4 design continued to be built after the Grouping of 1923, brick-based examples appearing at Hertford North and Bramley in 1924, Park Drain and Welwyn Garden City in 1926 and Blankney in 1928, and a modified version was classified by the Signalling Study Group as LNER Type 11.

Left (149):
Official elevations and plans of the new signalbox at Moorhouse. This is the earliest representation of the GNR's new standard signalbox, part of the changes introduced by A. Ross, the company's Engineer, and W. H. Cannon, the Signal Superintendent, after 1902. *John Cockcroft Collection*

Above left (150):
(Little) Bytham signalbox, photographed on 30 March 1970. The box was closed on 6 July 1975. *M. A. King*

Above right (151):
Official photograph of Loversall Carr signalbox shortly after it had opened in 1909. Unlike most other examples of this type of box, there were no locking room windows on the front elevation. The signalbox remained operational until 12 January 1975.
Peterborough Museum & Art Gallery

7. Single Lines

The GNR operated a number of single line branches (*Picture 152*) but many of them were run on behalf of independent companies. The majority of the shorter branches remained single all their working lives but where lines were used by through traffic and single line working began to cause congestion, they were converted to double track. References as to how the GNR operated its single lines are fragmentary, and this author has tried not to make assumptions where there is no evidence. If information appears to be incomplete or missing from the text, it is because it could not be found.

In the 1850s there is mention of both the electric telegraph and the use of the Train Staff, but no details. It is known that the latter was a wooden or metal baton with a flattened end appropriately lettered, to indicate that a driver had authority to pass over a certain section of track. The principle was that no train could travel between two stations without the Staff. However, when more than one train had to pass through a single line section in the same direction, the drivers of all but the last train were simply shown the Staff as their authority to proceed. The Board of Trade then made it a requirement that a ticket should be issued to every train crew not able to carry the Staff through the section, and eventually the GNR provided tickets on most of its single lines. In line with most other railway companies, the GNR used the terminology Train Staff and Train Ticket to describe this way of working. By 1874, all the GNR's single lines used the Train Staff system of working and later, both the electric telegraph and the absolute block system were used in addition. The latter worked in exactly the same way as it did on double track lines and is described in detail in Chapter 3.

By the beginning of the 20th century, most single lines were protected by standard block instruments and bells and the Train Staff and Train Ticket system, in line with Board of Trade recommendations (*Picture 153*). Some branches worked with only the Train Staff, while others operated with one engine in steam and Train Staff. Logically it was unnecessary to provide a Staff if there was only ever one engine at work on a branch at a time but that is what is recorded in the appendices to the Working Timetables. All these methods were quite adequate for the traffic demands on most of the GNR's branches and the company never felt the need to install the LNWR's design of Electric Train Staff, which was marketed by the Railway Signal Co and became popular with a number of railway companies from the 1890s. It was not until the first years of the 20th century that the company used Tyer's Electric Tablet System, although it had been available since the mid-1870s. Even then, it was introduced on only three branches — Willoughby-Mablethorpe, the Stanton Branch and the Enfield Extension.

Traffic demands were undoubtedly the reason for installation of Tyer's equipment, but considering the conservatism of the previous century, the use of permissive tablet working on the Enfield Extension in 1918 was all the more startling, especially as the installation was unique in this country at the time. After that, Hill the Engineer had no compunction in suggesting the use of Tyer's Intermediate Tablet Instruments during the November 1920 deliberations on how to control the new crossing loop at Burton Lane on the recently opened single line from High Dyke (on the main line, five miles south of Grantham) to Stainby.

This chapter examines the signalling history of a number of single lines in chronological order according to when they were opened. (NB: only lines for which the signalling history is known are included here.)

Horncastle (August 1855)

The Horncastle & Kirkstead Junction Railway opened its single track line on 11 August 1855 and from that date until the Grouping of 1923 it was worked by the GNR. Some time in 1877 the electric telegraph was installed to supplement the Train Staff system and in July 1888 a fully interlocked signalbox was brought into use at Woodhall Spa. Another was provided at Horncastle station as part of the resignalling there at the end of 1890. The branch was then worked as two sections by absolute block and Train Staff and Train Ticket systems. The resignalling cost £1,530 and as the Horncastle Company was unable to afford this expenditure, the GNR's Traffic Committee agreed in July 1892 that it should pay interest on the outlay at 4% per annum.

Stamford & Essendine (November 1856)

This short single track line was promoted by Lord Exeter and initially worked by the GNR for 50% of gross receipts. Although the line was operated until its closure as a single track, a second line of rails was laid within three years of its opening, but as the Railway Inspectorate was unhappy with the arrangements at Essendine and because the line was not the most remunerative, the doubling was never completed.

During 1877 the electric telegraph was installed but it was not until April 1886 that the General Manager wrote to the company stating:

'I think the time has now arrived when we must institute block working on the Stamford line but as it will necessitate an expenditure of about £100 to £150 I have on behalf of my Directors to ask your Company's approval of the outlay. As you are aware the Board of Trade now require block working to be instituted on all lines, single, as well as double, and as there are five occasions per day when there are two engines on the Stamford line at the same time, it is I think expedient to provide this protection with the view to prevent accidents...'

Included in the calculations was the price of block instruments and bells for a new 'movable' box at Ryhall, described as of the type used as temporary signalboxes on the East Lincolnshire line.

Barkston Junction and Boston (June 1857-April 1859)

This single track line had been built by the Boston, Sleaford & Midland Counties Railway, operated by the GNR from the start and then absorbed by it on 1 January 1865. The first section between Barkston and Sleaford opened on 13 June 1857. When Captain Tyler inspected the extension to Boston for the Board of Trade in March 1859, he would not sanction opening until the electric telegraph had been installed. This was completed by his return and when the line opened throughout on 12 April 1859, it was recorded that two Train Staffs of different shapes and colours were used to divide the route into two sections. This was probably the first use of the Train Staff on the GNR.

The branch was eventually converted into a double track line in an extraordinarily piecemeal fashion, as the following information clearly shows:

Table 28. Doubling of the single Barkston Junction to Boston line 1866-81

Barkston to Honington	1 February 1866
Honington to Ancaster	1 December 1873
Ancaster to Wilsford	9 May 1881
Wilsford to Broadwater (Rauceby)	1 December 1880
Broadwater (Rauceby) to Sleaford	29 July 1880
Sleaford to Heckington	1 June 1878
Heckington to Swineshead	1 May 1877
Swineshead to Hubberts Bridge	22 March 1880
Hubberts Bridge to Boston	31 May 1879

Hatfield & Hertford (March 1858)

Built by the Welwyn & Hertford Railway and opened to passengers on 1 March 1858, this single track line was worked jointly by the GNR and the Eastern Counties Railway. Originally the branch joined the GNR at Welwyn Junction, the site of the 1920s Welwyn Garden City station, but in 1876 the branch was extended alongside the up main line for two miles to Hatfield station and Welwyn Junction was abolished.

The electric telegraph was brought into use in 1877 and in December 1885 the Way & Works Committee gave its approval to installation of the block system on the branch at an estimated cost of £214. It also noted that extra signalmen would be needed at Hertford. The only section not protected by block working was the short stretch between Hertford GN and Hertford GE stations. Following the passing of the 1889 Regulation of Railways Act, the GNR was forced to upgrade the signalling again and in November the Way & Works Committee noted that a new passing place was required at Cole Green station.

Hatfield, Luton & Dunstable (May 1858 and September 1860)

The Hertford, Luton & Dunstable Railway Co, which built this line, incorporated the Welwyn & Hertford Railway noted above. The single track line from a junction with the LNWR at Dunstable to Luton was opened to passengers on 3 May 1858 and the remainder of the line to Welwyn Junction was opened to passengers on

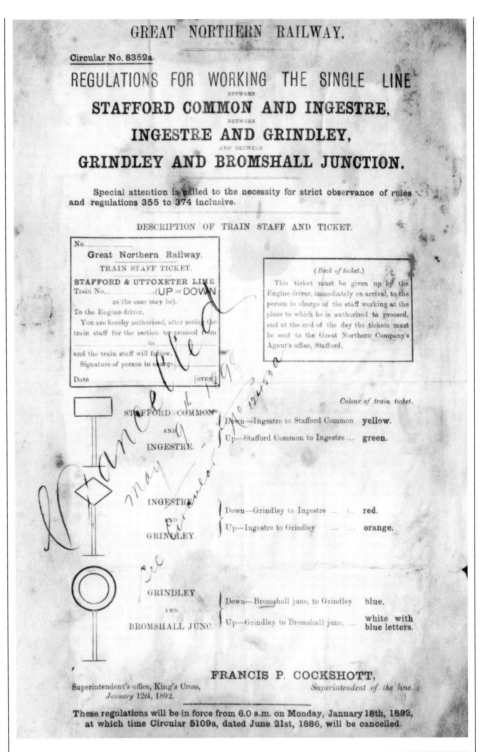

1 September 1860, from which time the GNR took over its operation. In June the following year the company was absorbed by the GNR and following various improvements, Train Staff working (no tickets) was introduced from 16 October 1865.

In the first months of 1869 the branch was extended southwards alongside the main line for just over two miles to Hatfield station and this meant considerable alteration to the signalling at the station. Col Hutchinson went to inspect the works in January and commented that it was '...a pity the company applied for an inspection before they were completed, which is at present by no means the case'. It was not until November that year that he was content with the arrangements in 'Hatfield North Junction Signal Box' and allowed the extension to be used.

Absolute block working was introduced on the branch on Wednesday 28 March 1877, when eight new signalboxes were opened. Ayot was one of these but when the Railway Inspectorate visited this station in the spring of 1881, it was not happy with what it saw. There was only one platform on the single line and no passing place, no runaway points despite the steep gradient, and the points into the goods loop operated from the signalbox were 215 yards from the box, when the Board of Trade requirements specified that facing points should be no more than 150 yards away from a signalbox. Inspector Marindin demanded meeting chaired by Thomas Hughes MP on 8 November, at least 55 signalmen who worked between King's Cross and Hitchin signed a memorial asking for a standard eight-hour working day as well as 30 shillings per week for 'Junction men' and 26s per week for 'Straight road men'[16]. Seymour Clarke the General Manager wrote to a number of other railway companies for details of their rates of pay and conditions and the accompanying table is a collation of the facts he put to the GNR Board in February 1866.

The Press reported the GNR dispute and the issue became public. One of the allegations was that men were being forced to work 18-hour shifts. Cockshott, the Superintendent of the Line, countered this by claiming that this was what the men themselves had wanted when changing shift patterns on a Sunday. However, he was prepared to alter the procedure to make it just six hours if '...a signalman who has been a month on day duty viz from 6am to 6pm must on a Sunday when he changes duty go off at 12 noon and be replaced by the Signalman who had been a month on night duty, the former will then resume duty at 6pm and take his month of night work.'

In February 1866 Clarke reluctantly reported to the Board that he wished to change the 'Gas Works Signals' at King's Cross from a two to a three shift job but the dispute rumbled on and at the end of March 1866, 36 signalmen in the Leeds District signed a petition for an extra 5s per week, followed in May by 17 Doncaster signalmen asking for a similar increase. In June the Board agreed to raise the wages of signalmen in the Yorkshire District by 1s per week. This took First Class signalmen's pay to 22s in their first year, 23s in their second, and 24s in their third year. Second Class signalmen's wages in their first year rose to 20s, to 21s in the second year and finally to 22s in the third year '...with £5 bonus subject to the usual regulations'. As for London signalmen, the Board returned the problem to the General Manager and Superintendent of the Line, asking them to use their own discretion in the hours to be worked.

With the extension of block working and the building of hundreds of new fully interlocked signalboxes in the 1870s and 80s, the number and status of signalmen increased enormously (Picture 171). In 1861 the GNR employed 150 signalmen, by the middle of the 1880s the number had risen to 907 and by 1897 the total was 1,284.

[16] The nature of the signatures on this petition implies that all these men were fully literate and had some standard of education.

Portfolio, Leen Valley Junction

GREAT NORTHERN RAILWAY.

SIGNALMEN'S HOURS OF DUTY.

Circular No. 2,232 a.

The Directors have agreed that each Signalman shall, when it is practicable, be relieved from duty every alternate Sunday, and when such cannot be arranged he shall be paid extra for the day's work. The following arrangements are now in force, viz. :—

At all Twelve Hours Signal Boxes the Signalmen are to relieve each other from duty at 7.0 a.m. and 7.0 p.m., and the change from day to night duty is to be effected as follows, viz. :—

The man leaving duty at 7.0 a.m. to return at 1.0 p.m., and remain until 7.0 p.m.

The man taking charge at 7.0 a.m. to go off duty at 1.0 p.m., and resume duty for the night at 7.0 p.m.

Each Twelve Hours Signalman to have twenty-four consecutive hours off duty on alternate Sundays, when he has been on duty daily throughout the preceding fortnight. When he cannot be relieved from alternate Sunday duty, but is required to work fourteen days in a fortnight, he is to be paid one day overtime.

The days on which the Twelve Hours duty men are to change from day to night will be fixed by the Superintendent of the Line and posted in the respective Signal Boxes.

At Eight Hours Signal Boxes the Signalmen are to relieve each other from duty at 6.0 a.m., 2.0 p.m., and 10.0 p.m. respectively, except at the end of each week, when they will change duty thus—

No. 1 on duty from 10.0 p.m. Saturday to 6.0 a.m. Sunday.
   „ 2 „ „   6.0 a.m. Sunday to 2.0 p.m.   „
   „ 1 „ „   2.0 p.m.   „   10.0 „   „
   „ 2 „ „   10.0 „   „   6.0 a.m. Monday.
   „ 3 „ „   6.0 a.m. Monday to 2.0 p.m.   „,
or by dividing the 24 hours from 6.0 a.m. Sunday to 6.0 a.m. Monday into two terms of duty of twelve hours each, instead of three of eight hours each.

The Signalmen at any Eight Hours Box, having selected one of these plans for changing duty on Sundays, must not alter the hours without the authority of the Superintendent of the Line.

The men at Eight Hours Boxes who do the Sunday work, and who have not had eight hours' relief from duty during the preceding six days, will each be paid an extra half-day's wage.

When an Eight Hours' Signalman is required to do temporary duty at a Twelve Hours Box, his wages will be paid as per day of twelve hours.

When a Relief Signalman or a Signalman of a Twelve Hours Box, is required to take duty at an Eight Hours Box he will be paid wages at eight hours per day.

Circular No. 2208a is cancelled.

FRANCIS P. COCKSHOTT,
Superintendent of the Line.

King's Cross,
17th January, 1879.

Table 32. Comparative rates of signalmen's pay per week, 1866

	London	Bonus	Country	Bonus
First Class				
GNR	23s-25s	£10 (a year)	21s-23s	£10 (a year)
MR	19s-21s	none		
GWR	26s	£5	20s-22s	£2/3 or £5
			(at one or two important signal places in the country, 26s is paid)	
The GWR give three days holiday yearly and pay the men's wages during that time.				
Second Class				
GNR	21s-23s	£10	19s-21s	£5
MR	18s-20s	none		
No Classes Specified				
LNWR	19s-23s	£3	19s-23s	none
GER	20s-25s	none	17s-21s	none
NER			17s-22s	none
NLR	21s-25s	none		
(Every NLR signalman worked a three shift pattern.)				

Above (171):
This particular copy of circular No 2,232a of 17 January 1879, informing signalmen of their hours of duty, was pasted into the 'portfolio' at Leen Valley Junction signalbox in Nottinghamshire. The signalmen there kept their portfolio up to date and in March 1912 pasted in the latest employment conditions: an 8-hour day; 48-hour working week; six days paid holiday a year; the bonus system discontinued and replaced with weekly wages of 28s (£1.40) first year, 29s (£1.45) second year, and 30s (£1.50) third year; Sundays, Christmas Day and Good Friday to be paid at time and a quarter. *Author's Collection*

In view of these statistics and the effect it had on the wages bill, it is not surprising that the Board retained a tight control over terms and conditions, and liaised with other railway companies to maintain the status quo by mutual consent. What few trade unions there were in this period had no influence with management, and central government only became directly involved following an accident on the NER at Thirsk on 2 November 1892. James Holmes, a signalman at Manor House signalbox between Northallerton and Thirsk, had pronounced himself unfit to go on duty due to lack of sleep brought about by attending to his sick daughter who subsequently died, and coping with his distraught wife. But no relief could be found, and waking up confused after having fallen asleep on duty, he allowed an express into an already occupied section. Holmes was charged with the manslaughter of a guard who was one of nine fatalities in the ensuing crash, but the details that emerged during his trial caused a public outcry. Although he was found guilty by a York jury, he was discharged and released by the Judge.

Henry Oakley immediately compiled a report for his Board, anticipating government legislation to reduce signalmen's hours, and the contents of this report contain some interesting details. Of the 1,090 signalmen employed by the company, 721 worked 12-hour shifts and the remaining 369 worked eight hours. Oakley wrote:

'...if the company felt compelled to increase the eight hour boxes, those lines where express trains run at speed and where the work is continuous and heavy, should be the first selected, and would be covered by —

The *main line* from London to Leeds and Bradford inclusive:

to *convert* the existing twelve hour boxes to eight hour for this section only will require 127 additional men, at an estimated annual cost of £7,958.

The *West Riding* line will also require 20 additional men, estimated to cost £1,207.

The *Grantham & Nottingham* branch on which fast trains run, will need about 15 men at a cost of £940.'

The Board of Trade report into the Thirsk accident was published in January 1893 and a 10-hour maximum working day was recommended for all signalmen throughout the country. The ensuing Regulation of Railways Act 1893, however, did not go as far as enforcing this. The Board of Trade was encouraged to put pressure on a railway company to alter shift patterns if a complaint had been made by employees of that railway about '...excessive hours, insufficient rest, or insufficient relief of Sundays'. Section 1 (iii) of the Act continued: 'The amended schedule of hours may be enforced by the Railway & Canal Commissioners.'

When the GNR's General Manager reported to the Board in March 1894, he confirmed that a reduction of hours had been achieved on '...practically nearly the whole of the main line', the cost of the alterations increasing expenditure by £8,000 per annum. This was just as well, because in November that year, the Railway Clearing House called a meeting of all general managers to consider the Board of Trade's intention to refer the GER to the Railway Commissioners for not reducing signalmen's hours on certain parts of its system.

As time passed, however, the railway companies began to resist the Board of Trade pressure to reduce hours, and the GNR made its stand in July 1896. Having received a letter from the Board of Trade drawing attention to the remaining 12-hour shifts at signalboxes between Holme and Tallington and suggesting that four 10-hour shifts should be reduced to eight hours, the General Manager told the GNR Board that it should make no changes, and that '...in the event of the case being remitted to the Railway Commissioners, the assistance of all the other railway companies could be obtained in support of the Company's view...'

One of the outcomes of this appears to have been a wage rise, presumably to discourage employees from complaining to the Board of Trade. Early in 1897, 504 signalmen had their weekly wages increased by between 1s and 3s, but unfortunately for the General Manager, this was not the end of the matter, and he had to allow a deputation from the men to discuss further concessions. Another meeting took place at King's Cross on 13 January the following year.

By 1907 disputes were so common that the Board of Trade suggested 'conciliation boards' should be formed. The GNR created four 'boards' in October the following year, one of which discussed signalmen's, guards' and shunters' grievances. Agreement could not always be reached and, in 1909, a major dispute was submitted to Lord MacDonell for arbitration. The outcome was improved wages and conditions for signalmen and other staff.

Telegraph Boys

Within a year of the block system being operational along the whole of the main line, it was found necessary at signalboxes with large lever frames to relieve the signalmen of the task of sending and receiving messages on the 'speaking' telegraph instruments. Judging by the language used in the Traffic Committee minutes of its meeting of 5 February 1873, the first appointments of Telegraph Boys were made that year at Spital Junction, Peterborough. Three Lad Porters were employed there solely to work the instruments because '...the new Locking Frame fitted to this Box necessitated so much additional attention, that the Signalmen have no time for the performance of this duty'. From that date onwards the number of 'Telegraph Boys', or 'Lads', continued to grow as traffic increased. As just one of many examples, telegraph lads were appointed to Sleaford East and West signalboxes in June 1882 and the signalmen there upgraded from third to second class, because of the extra work brought about by the opening of the GN&GE Joint Railway that year.

Discipline and Reward

As explained in Chapter 1, the Executive & Traffic Committee and its two successors dealt mainly with staff issues and it is from the minutes of their meetings that the following information has been gleaned. As might be expected, discipline was as important to the GNR as to all the other railway companies.

Any employee not adhering to the Rules and Regulations could expect swift and uncompromising punishment. The worst transgressions could lead to dismissal. In 1853, Robert Laing, a signalman at Grantham, was dismissed for '...allowing a train to pass his signals contrary to instructions and thereby endangering the lives of passengers on the 11th February'. Tiredness was obviously a problem in the early years, and the staff at Peterborough had a particularly bad reputation. In July 1853, William Marshall, a signalman there, was sacked for being drunk and asleep on duty and 10 months later in May 1854, his colleague William Mills was also dismissed for being asleep. Fortunately for Thomas Cann of Peterborough, dismissal was not always the automatic punishment for such a misdemeanour and although he delayed a local train in March 1855 by not staying awake, he was only suspended.

Demotion and the consequent reduction of pay was another option which appears to have been used, not just as a punishment but as a more humane way of dealing with what the company believed was a genuine mistake. After a 'slight accident' at Welwyn North Tunnel on 4 December 1869, for example, the Executive Committee recorded that: 'The accident arose in consequence of a mistake made by the Signalman at Welwyn station, Clarke, who is an old servant, and has hitherto borne an excellent character but who on this occasion in absence of mind lowered the Down Signal, although the Down instrument shewed "Train on Line".'

Clarke was reduced to a porter and benefited from the caring face of the company, whereas signalman Henderson's demotion to porter in March 1879 for not keeping his signalbox clean seems somewhat severe.

Demotion could sometimes be a personal decision, as was the case with Signalman Birkett of Retford, who decided in February 1875 that he would prefer to be a gatekeeper at Newark rather than try and master the new 60-lever frame in the recently opened Retford North signalbox.

Fines were another means of encouraging staff not to err. When Porter Day started the fire which destroyed Littleworth signalbox on 7 August 1881, because contrary to the regulations he had been lighting the level crossing gate lamps in the locking room, he was fined 5s.

As well as punishments, the GNR also had a number of ways to reward its staff. The most common form of staff incentive was a scheme of regular bonuses for good conduct, which was operated from at least the 1850s. Although payment was never automatic, as long as an employee had not broken any rules or been absent longer than was allowed within a set period, for most these bonuses became predictable supplements to their income. From time to time, however, some hard decisions had to be made, such as that made by the Executive Committee at its 6 December 1877 meeting. Signalman Gooding was 13 days short of the period necessary to entitle him to his Good Conduct bonus, but as his absence from work had been caused by having been struck by lightning while on duty, the Committee agreed that he should receive it none the less.

Rewards were completely at the discretion of the committees, as was the case in June 1867, when the Traffic Committee agreed with the General Manager that after 16 years' unblemished service and 23 bonuses, Signalman Baggett of Doncaster, '...who is now no longer competent for a Signalman's duty, be allowed to take charge of Finningley Gate at his present pay of 12s a week'.

Extra payments were occasionally made for bravery and sometimes in addition to sick pay following accidents. After Signalman Milner Houlden had been seriously injured falling from a bridge at Welwyn whilst carrying out his work on 25 September 1856, the Executive & Traffic Committee agreed to make up the difference between his sick pay — 12s per week — and his normal wages — 20s per week. In December 1870, Signalman Jonas Samworth was awarded £5, because his '...coolness and prompt action...' prevented an accident at New England on 12 October that year.

Personalities

In such a large staff involved with the signalling of the railway there must have been many memorable characters, the majority of whom have left no record in the official company documentation. The GNR had its fair share of employees who earnestly worked their way up through the ranks from humble origins to more elevated positions and inevitably they did leave a mark. Richard Johnson, the company's Engineer, was perhaps the most notable example (see Chapter 1), but there were others. Edward French, Hitchin's signal fitter responsible for the design of the GNR's somersault signal, is referred to in Chapter 4. Amos Piggott [17] started his career on the GNR as a pointsman at Newark in 1852 at a weekly salary of 19s and in 1859 he became Signal Inspector based at Retford. In 1873 he backed the development of John Thomas's oil lamp, a patent for which was deposited jointly by the two men — see Chapter 4. Piggott eventually

[17] Piggott was born at Varlow Vantage in Berkshire in 1827 or 1828.

rose to the rank of Chief Signal Inspector based at Retford and when he was forced to retire in May 1893 due to ill health, '...the Directors in order to mark their appreciation of his long and faithful service...' awarded him a year's pay — £250. To put this gesture into perspective, his replacement, William Hill, who until then had been the station master at Laisterdyke, was appointed on probation, at £150pa plus 17s 6d a week expenses.

The perseverance of other lesser characters sometimes shows in the company's records by default. For example, after a serious accident at Peterborough on 13 January 1880, E. Lawrence was fitted with an artificial leg. He returned to work as a signalman at New England and by July 1883 the Executive Committee agreed to supply him with a replacement, as the original one was '...shewing signs of failure'. Mr Lawrence remained active, so much so that by April 1895 this limb was '...worn out' and once again the company agreed to pay for a new one.

Staff Training

Quite how signalmen learnt their jobs in the early days is not fully understood. Those who could read would no doubt have studied the rule book which was issued to all staff, and have learnt the practicalities 'on the job'. For example, it was reported that while Thomas Giles had been a policeman at Newark in 1854, he had been

'learning signals', and as a result was promoted to signalman at Grantham at 21s a week, an increase of 3s, which was a considerable rise at that time.

The first reference to a more formal method of training of signalmen comes from the minutes of the Traffic Committee's meeting of 6 May 1880, when policeman Keys of Peterborough was seeking compensation for being struck on the head by a lamp in the Signal Learners' Room at King's Cross back in 1874. There was another similar establishment at Retford, the earliest reference to it appearing in March 1877, when 100,000 old bricks and 2,000 old slates were to be obtained for £49 10s, either to extend an existing facility, or build a completely new one (*Picture 172*). It has not been possible to discover whether or not each District or Division had its own Signal Learners' Room, because there are very few direct references to training in the company archives. One of the few, minuted at a Traffic Committee meeting during the spring of 1896, simply recorded that because there was a staff shortage, the number of 'Signal Learners' had been increased from 20 to 30.

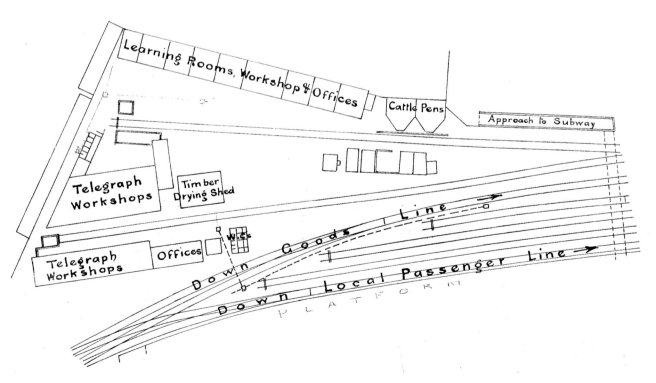

G.N.R. RETFORD.

Proposed W.C.'s &c. for Signal Learners.

Scale, 50 feet to an inch.

SIGNAL ALTERATIONS.

KING'S CROSS WEST.

Wᴇ

Starting signal from No. 1 departure line, fixed over No. 1 departure line under Battle bridge (existing signal) ...

Fixed over platform line "E," on south girder of Battle bridge (existing signal).
1. Starting Platform line "E" western route ... ... 1 crow
2. „ „ „ „ eastern „ 1 crow, pause, 1 crow

West of platform line "C," immediately south of Battle bridge (existing signal).
1. „ Platform line "C" western route 5
2. „ „ „ „ eastern „ ... ... 1 long
3. „ „ „ "D" western „ ... ... 3 crow
4. „ „ „ „ eastern „ ... ... 2 long

West of coal stage line, 20 yards south of Battle bridge (existing signal).
1. „ Coal stage line western route 4
2. „ „ „ „ eastern „ ... ... 4 crow
3. „ Engine line western route ... ... 2 „
4. „ „ „ eastern „ ... ... 3 short

Fixed over suburban line under Battle bridge (existing signal).
1. „ Suburban line "B" to down slow line ... 3
2. „ „ „ „ western route ... 2

West of "A" platform line, immediately south of Battle bridge (existing signal).
1. Platform line "A' or western sidings to down slow line 1 long, 3 short
2. „ „ „ „ „ „ „ „ main No. 2 1 „ 2 „
3. „ „ „ „ „ „ „ „ „ 1 1 „

Directing signal over departure lines, and affixed to west box, immediately south of Congreve St. bridge (existing signal).
1. Western route to down slow line ... ... 5 short
2. „ „ „ „ main „ No. 2 ... ... 3 crow
3. „ „ „ „ „ „ „ 1 ... ... 2 long
4. Eastern „ „ „ „ „ 1 1 long, pause, 1 long
5. No. 1 departure to down main line, No. 2 ... 1 long, 1 short
6. „ 1 „ „ „ „ „ 1 1
7. Nos. 1, 2 and 3 sidings to down main line No. 1 By shunters' instructions
8. „ „ „ „ „ „ northern spur ... ... Do.
9. No. 2 departure to down main line, No. 2 2
10. „ 2 „ „ „ „ „ 1 1
11. „ 2 „ „ northern spur By shunters' instructions

East of up carriage line and immediately south of gas works tunnel (existing signal).
1. No. 1 down main line to down goods advance 3
2. „ 1 „ „ „ advance 1

No. 2 Down main line advance, east of No. 2 down main line, opposite last-named post (existing signal) 2

Fixed to retaining wall, opposite last-named post.
1. Down slow to down goods line advance... 4
2. „ „ line advance 3

Trains passing from No. 1 departure platform line to down main line No. 2 must not run over the crossover road at a higher rate of speed than 8 miles per hour.

Special Orders and Circulars

By the 1860s, communication between management and staff about operational matters was via Special Orders. The earliest surviving was issued by Seymour Clarke from King's Cross on 21 November 1864. It warned staff of the Traffic and Engineers' Department not to work on the permanent way or remove rails without first informing the 'Semaphore Signalman' and getting him to place his signals at danger.

Some time between Cockshott's appointment as Superintendent of the Line in 1865 and Henry Oakley succeeding Clarke as General Manager in 1870, Special Orders were replaced by printed Circulars. These were issued from King's Cross by these managers' respective offices, and each was consecutively numbered. The earliest that survives from the Superintendent of the Line's office is No 355a of 30 July 1870, and the latest is No 28,397a issued on 19 September 1913. From 1 January 1875 'Guard Books' or 'Portfolios' were issued to every signalbox, and onto the blank pages of these bound books the circulars were pasted. Circulars with general information such as procedures to be adopted during fogs and snow storms (No 617a, 6 January 1877), or the use of signal and point lever stops on lever frames (No 11,620a, January 1897) went to all signalboxes. Those of a specific nature, for example the opening of a new signalbox at Mapperley in the Nottinghamshire District on 31 October 1899 (No 13,681a), were probably only distributed to the signalboxes in that District. After 1902 when the post of Superintendent of the Line was abolished, circulars continued to be issued by W. H. Hills in his capacity as Superintendent of a new Running Department, and then when the Superintendent of the Line's office was reinstated in May 1910, Hills' name continued to appear in that capacity (Pictures 173a and b and 174a and b).

Circulars were also issued jointly by various departments and some of these appear to have had their own numbering sequence. For example, on 10 March 1881 Francis Cockshott, Superintendent of the Line, and James Radcliffe, Telegraph Superintendent, put their names to

Above left (173a):
Part of Circular No 12,742a, issued on 18 August 1898 by J. Alexander, Superintendent of the Line, informing staff of the alteration and renaming of lines between King's Cross West and Belle Isle Down signalboxes, and of the new up carriage line between the terminus and Belle Isle Up signalbox. *Great Northern Railway Society*

Left (173b):
4-4-2 No 1441, signalled out of Departure Platform No 1 at King's Cross and on to the down main, at the end of the first decade of the 20th century. By this time Congreve Street Bridge, mentioned in Circular No 12,742a, had been removed but Battle Bridge Road bridge (just visible in the background) still straddled the tracks just north of the train shed. Shortly after this photograph was taken, the brackets supporting the departure signals shown here were replaced by an impressive metal lattice structure (see pic 17a).
Locomotive Publishing Co

Right (174a):
Circular No 10,436a, dated 18 June 1895.
Great Northern Railway Society

GREAT NORTHERN RAILWAY.

Circular No. 10,436a.

NEW FACING CONNECTION DOWN MAIN TO DOWN SLOW LINE
WOOD GREEN BOX 1.

SIGNAL ALTERATIONS.

HORNSEY BOX 3.

The position of the signals on the down signal bridge at Hornsey box No. 3 will be altered and made as below:—

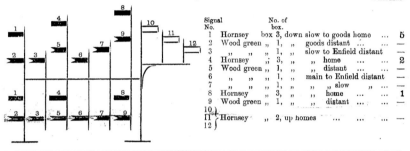

WHISTLES.

Signal No.	No. of box.			
1	Hornsey box 3, down slow to goods home	...	...	5
2	Wood green „ 1, „ goods distant	...	...	—
3	„ „ „ 1, „ slow to Enfield distant		...	—
4	Hornsey „ 3, „ „ home	...	...	2
5	Wood green „ 1, „ „ distant	...	...	—
6	„ „ „ 1, „ main to Enfield distant		...	—
7	„ „ „ 1, „ „ „ slow „	...	—
8	Hornsey „ 3, „ „ home	...	...	1
9	Wood green „ 1, „ „ distant	...	...	—
10				
11	Hornsey „ 2, up homes			—
12				

WOOD GREEN BOX 1.

The signals on down signal bridge at Wood green box No. 1 will be altered and made as below, viz :—

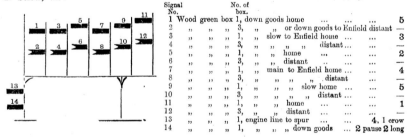

Signal No.	No. of box.			
1	Wood green box 1, down goods home			5
2	„ „ „ 3, „ „ or down goods to Enfield distant			—
3	„ „ „ 1, „ slow to Enfield home ...		...	3
4	„ „ „ 3, „ „ „ distant...		...	—
5	„ „ „ 1, „ home		...	2
6	„ „ „ 3, „ distant ...		...	—
7	„ „ „ 1, „ main to Enfield home ...		...	4
8	„ „ „ 3, „ „ „ distant		...	—
9	„ „ „ 1, „ „ „ slow home ...		...	5
10	„ „ „ 3, „ „ „ distant ...		...	—
11	„ „ „ 1, „ „ home ...		...	1
12	„ „ „ 3, „ „ distant ...		...	—
13	„ „ „ 1, engine line to spur		4, 1 crow	
14	„ „ „ 1, „ „ „ down goods ...		2 pause 2 long	

In use from noon on Sunday, 23rd June, 1895.

FRANCIS P. COCKSHOTT,
Superintendent of the line.

(90,830)

KING'S CROSS,
June 18th, 1895.
(1,750)

Circular No 285a, listing the signalboxes and telegraph offices that would receive the 10am transmission of Greenwich Time from King's Cross, and giving instructions as to who would transmit this time on to other signalboxes and offices. This circular cancelled one that had been in force since 28 August 1872. The Superintendent of the Line and the Locomotive Engineer also produced joint circulars, an example being No 12,125a issued by J. Alexander and H.A. Ivatt on 4 October 1897, giving engine drivers a list of all the sections of line controlled by the permissive block system. In some cases, the Superintendent of the Line, the Locomotive Engineer and the Chief Engineer put their names to circulars, for example No 617a, issued as a direct result of the Abbotts Ripton accident of January 1876 (see Chapter 4), detailing the actions to be taken by signalmen during 'fogs and snow storms'. Where the GNR had junctions with other railways, circulars were issued jointly by the two companies.

As well as circulars, the GNR also issued 'Notices of Signal Alterations, Relaying and other Permanent Way Operations, Repairs to Bridges, Tunnels, Signal and Interlocking Apparatus, &c' to its operational staff. As examples of what these small leaflets contained, for the period Sunday 4 April to Saturday 10 April (midnight) 1897, drivers were warned that at Hatfield signalboxes were being painted, single line working was in operation on the down line between St Neots and Tempsford on Sunday 4th, and the up slow distant signal arm and lamp at Red Hall had been lowered to 17ft and 14 ft 6in respectively. In the Lincolnshire District during the same period, the levers in West Street signalbox, Boston, were to be 'rearranged' on Sunday 4th, while in the West Riding Yorkshire District, a new miniature signal was being fixed at the exit of Quarry Siding connecting to Mr Akeroyd's Soothill Colliery at Woodkirk.

The Telegraph Department at Retford, by comparison, does not appear to have issued circulars or special notices, but relied on its communication by duplicated memoranda, either completely hand-written, hand-written on printed forms or printed and partly completed by hand.

Rules & Regulations, Working Timetables and Appendices

Underpinning the work of everyone on the railway were the Rules and Regulations. The earliest comprehensive GNR rule book, described as General Instructions, was published in 1850. This was supplied to all staff, but more specific and detailed instructions, such as how to operate the block telegraph system, (see Chapter 3) were issued separately to signalling staff as Regulations. Every railway company had its own set of Rules & Regulations and it took many years before these were finally brought into line. In 1867 the General Managers' Conference agreed on certain standards and the GNR revised its 1855 Rule Book accordingly. At the end of 1874 an all-railway companies' committee was set up to try and improve on these standards, and the changes were approved in 1876. But it was not until a serious accident on the GNR in

December 1881 that a concerted effort was made to complete the standardisation process. Within the space of an hour there was a series of accidents in Canonbury Tunnel because the seven-stroke bell code tapped out by the North London Railway signalman to signify 'line temporarily blocked' according to his company's Regulations, was interpreted by the GNR signalman receiving them according to his company's Regulations as permissive working. As a direct result of this misunderstanding, 17 basic bell codes including, most importantly, emergency ones, were finally agreed between all British railway companies. The GNR notified its signalling staff in Circular No 4388a, 29 September 1884, that new Block Working Regulations would come into force at 1pm on Sunday 5 October 1884, 'the object being to cancel the several varying codes in use on the different Railways... The sheets of old rules must be removed from the Signalboxes and destroyed, and the mounted cards sent, on Sunday next, to the Signal Inspector, Retford.'

Further agreement on standard block working regulations was reached between all companies early in 1895, the GNR adopting them on 31 March that year, and by the beginning of the new century, all railways were using 33 standard 'Regulations for Working the Absolute Block Telegraph on Double Lines'.[18] It was a few more years before the standard British railways Rule Book appeared, the GNR issuing its first edition on 1 May 1904.

A vital supplement to the Rules & Regulations was a document which the GNR and many other railway companies termed the Appendix to the Working Timetables. The earliest GNR issue was published in 1881 and it contained a list of all the company's signalboxes, their opening hours and any special instructions concerned with their operation. Among a host of other detail, it also included the block telegraph regulations for absolute, single line and permissive ('Stop and Caution') working. These appendices became substantial documents, reflecting the complexity and ultimately the inflexibility of railway operation, the GNR's 1905 edition, for example, running to 302 pages.

[18] From Regulation 34 onwards, railways were free to make their own decisions. For example, Regulation 34 on the GNR concerned shunting, on the NER it informed staff about the use of travelling cranes and on the L&YR it gave instructions about short section working. The GNR used Regulation No 35 to inform its staff on the lighting of signal lamps; the NER had no use for the number, but the L&YR used it to regulate the operation of show van and roundabout specials!

Index